The Fibre Man

Denis Burkitt has won world acclaim for two
astonishing feats of medical detection. He played
a major role in uncovering the causes and
pioneering the cure for a form of cancer in
children. He was also a key figure in confirming
the link between many of the killer diseases of
the Western world and the lack of fibre in our
diet.

Handicapped by the loss of an eye in
childhood, unremarkable at school, it was with
the decision to go where the need was greatest,
whatever the cost, that the adventure of his life
began . . .

THE FIBRE MAN

The life-story of Dr Denis Burkitt

Brian Kellock

A LION PAPERBACK
Tring · Belleville · Sydney

Copyright © 1985 Denis Burkitt and Brian Kellock

Published by
Lion Publishing plc
Icknield Way, Tring, Herts, England
ISBN 0 85648 583 7
Albatross Books
PO Box 320, Sutherland, NSW 2232, Australia
ISBN 0 86760 455 7

First edition 1985

Printed in Great Britain by
Cox and Wyman Ltd, Reading

Contents

CHAPTER 1

Early Days

Denis Burkitt's first experience of the surgeon's knife should have put him off medicine for life. He was seven years old. The year was 1918. And the scene was the drawing-room of the Burkitt home, Lawnakilla, in the Irish county of Fermanagh.

Through the window, the view south-west across the sloping lawns was towards the waters of Lough Erne and beyond to the distant Benaughlin and Cultiagh mountains. The town of Enniskillen lay a mile and a half to the south.

It was nearly midday as father carried first Denis and then his younger brother Robin down from their bedroom, still in their pyjamas. The settee had been covered with clean, white sheets by their mother the night before. Uncle Roland was now standing between it and a cloth-covered table.

As Denis took it all in, it slowly dawned on him that there had been a reason for his uncle peering down into their mouths the previous night after tea, reaching into each throat with a searching finger. So this was why they had been kept in bed till gone eleven.

He felt cheated. He had been told they were going on a journey and needed to rest. But no one said the transport would be an anaesthetic. Or that they would return minus their tonsils. More than sixty years later Denis, now a famous surgeon with many tonsilectomies to his credit, still shudders at the risk his uncle was taking.

With no nurse standing by, little could have been done if there had been a sudden obstruction, or excessive bleeding.

No wonder his mother stayed out of sight. And father, who had no love of anything medical, soon disappeared into the kitchen.

Uncle Roland, who was home on holiday from his medical practice in Kenya, was a first-class doctor and surgeon, the one doctor the white people around Nairobi called in when things were bad. Mother and father knew all that. The trouble was, he could be very persuasive and was not easily put off, once he had a new interest. This time it was tonsils — Denis's and Robin's in particular.

The doctor's legendary reputation amongst his patients in Africa did nothing to restore his nephews' confidence. In particular, it seems he believed in curing fevers by artificially lowering the patient's temperature. Stories abounded; from how he had suspended a fevered baby, naked in an open basket in a draughty doorway, and sprayed it with cold water, to the time he had driven a near-naked lady with a high temperature from the country into Nairobi, arriving with the doctor only half-dressed and the shivering lady wearing his clothes.

Years after the boys had recovered from the single-handed removal of their tonsils, they still remained afraid of this particular uncle. But today Denis remembers him with affection rather than fear. This tall and godly man, with a twinkle in his eye, who back in Kenya was never afraid to tell the Governor where he was going astray, had a great influence on Denis in his childhood and early student days.

Uncle Roland's godliness and singlemindedness, combined with a certain disregard for other people's opinions of him, were not uncommon qualities in the Burkitt family. It was these qualities above all which would lead Denis in later life to make his important discoveries, increasing the life-expectancy of a large number of African children and who-knows-how-many other people throughout the world.

Denis's paternal grandfather had these qualities too. As a young man, in the 1850s, Thomas Burkitt left his home in the south-east of Ireland, where a century before his family had come from England to settle as land-owners. He stayed for a while with an uncle in Toronto. While there, he had a religious experience which turned him into a convinced Presbyterian. He came home to Ireland an ordained minister.

That might have been acceptable in Canada. But in Ireland he soon found that to be any sort of nonconformist was socially taboo. His staunchly episcopalian family disagreed with his convictions. So again he packed his bags and left home, this time for a remote corner of Donegal.

As a young, itinerant Presbyterian minister, Thomas Burkitt entered a life of hardship and danger. His chapel was a corrugated hut in Killybegs, a fishing-village in southern Donegal. Visiting his small, scattered flock meant travelling over wild country by pony — a revolver always ready at his side.

Despite certain poverty he married Emma, an equally devout and committed nonconformist. Together they managed to raise a family of five boys and two girls — on porridge, potatoes, Latin and Greek. All the boys did well in life, working their own way through university. Every one of them, except Denis's father, who became a civil engineer, eventually went abroad to work.

Robert became an archaeologist in Guatemala. Roland was the unstoppable surgeon. Harold worked with the Indian Civil Service, becoming Provincial Governor of Madras. And, as an engineer in the Punjab, Frank constructed canals and bridges. The two sisters remained spinsters, one a teacher.

At the time Denis was born, in February 1911, his father was County Surveyor, responsible for constructing and maintaining the roads and bridges in Fermanagh. As Denis and Robin grew up, they often went out with their father, taking turns to hold the theodolite as he laid routes for new roads across the mountains.

Denis's father was a practical man. No plumber or electrician ever needed to call at Lawnakilla, the house near Enniskillen where Denis spent the first fifteen years of his life, or at Laragh, three miles from Ballinamallard, where the family moved in 1926.

James Burkitt combined practical skills with a reluctance to spend money unnecessarily. No doubt he remembered the hard days of his manse childhood and did not want them repeated.

At Lawnakilla, where water had to be pumped by hand from a well 100 yards from the house, he constructed a metal cart to carry the daily supply. This was improved on at Laragh, where a petrol pump was adapted to deliver water directly to the house. Electricity came from batteries charged by a diesel engine, supplemented by oil-lamps.

Bath-water that barely covered his legs, and strict instructions to switch off lights when leaving a room, are memories of a way of life that made Denis a utility man, just like his father. Later in life, as he carried out exhaustive and highly rewarding research on a shoe-string budget, or made crutches for crippled Africans from discarded steel rods, he showed that money was not the first requirement for medical advance. Ideas and the ability to improvise were far more important.

As County Surveyor, Denis's father was responsible for some notable achievements. He constructed bridges to Boa Island on Lough Erne and introduced tarmacadam to Fermanagh. But it was as an amateur ornithologist that he became most famous and is most likely to be remembered.

He was the first naturalist to identify individual birds by putting metal bands of different patterns on the legs of robins. In this way he could plot their territories and distribution. He chose to use combinations of patterns for his rings rather than colour, because he was colour blind. In 1984, twenty-five years after his death, a small book was published under the title, *Ten Famous Irish Scientists*. Included were Robert Boyle, the father of modern chemistry; Lord Kelvin, the famous physicist; Ernest Walton, one of the team who first split the atom; William Hamilton, the mathematician who became president of the Royal Society; and James Muspratt, the chemist credited with the founding of the British alkali industry. Also included as one of the ten was James Parsons Burkitt, naturalist, who, in his final work on the behaviour of the robin, had written, 'I am thankful to have had this little bit of research into a corner of God's garden.'

Denis did not inherit his father's interest in birds, or his colour blindness. (He did, incidentally, inherit tone deafness.)

But his close and methodical approach to the geographical distribution of disease certainly bears evidence of his father's patient detective skill. There is also a remarkable similarity between the territorial sketches James Burkitt made of robins and other birds around the house at Lawnakilla and the maps produced by Denis half a century later, showing tumour distribution in Africa.

For the local people, an even stranger sight than James Burkitt stooping motionless in the corner of some field, waiting to catch a robin for ringing, was the family motor bike leaving Lawnakilla with the Burkitt family on board. The powerful Harley-Davidson had been skilfully modified by father. A sprung extension was added to the rear of the pillion to carry both boys. And the side-car was large enough to carry mother and their only sister, Peg, who was three years older than Denis. In the move to Laragh the motor bike was exchanged for a Model T Ford, one of the first to be seen around the roads of Enniskillen.

Life in Ireland in the 1920s was almost as troubled and divided as it is today. It was one of those times when 'the troubles' came to a head and there was rioting in the streets of Dublin. Although this had little effect on the Burkitt family, the social divisions between Protestant and Catholic were very marked. There was in fact no social contact between the two. There were Protestant shops and Catholic shops, Protestant clubs and Catholic clubs.

Social life for the Burkitts was also restricted by 'class'. Their friends were the dozen or so professional families — doctors, solicitors, clergy — who lived within convenient travelling distance of one another. There was a great deal of snobbery too. People in trade, no matter how rich, were somehow never quite accepted. The divisions between the established church and the nonconformists still went deep, and were felt right in the heart of the home. There were in fact so many barriers and prejudices that it is a wonder the Burkitt boys grew up with such a balanced view of the world.

Although he was the son of a Presbyterian minister, Denis's father adopted the Church of Ireland when he married

Gwendoline Hill. He eventually became churchwarden of Trory Parish Church as well as Sunday school teacher and the longest-serving member of the Synod of the Church of Ireland. But he was never confirmed.

Denis's mother was brought up in the established church and had a slightly condescending view of 'chapel folk'. At times she would deliberately needle her rather more intellectual husband, because he retained a degree of loyalty to his nonconformist upbringing. When that happened, he would go off and worship at some local Methodist church.

Despite the prejudices which were then a normal part of Irish life, both parents are remembered as godly people. Each morning they would have prayers after breakfast, just as their own parents had done before them, father reading from a brown-covered prayer book.

As boys, Denis and Robin were the best of friends, pretty well to the exclusion of anyone else. These were happy times of close friendship. School holidays were the best times, when they could get into the open air to play tennis, or camp on the moors, collecting sticks for a fire and with food out of tins. Once they had moved to Laragh, they were near a river and had their own boat. In the Easter holidays, especially, they would row down into Lough Erne. The islands in the lake made perfect camping and picnic sites.

The family spent much of the summer holiday in the small fishing-village of Mullaghmore, on the west coast — famous in more recent years as the place where Lord Mountbatten was killed. From the nearest station a jaunting-cart carried them to the village, where they stayed in a fisherman's cottage.

When Denis was nine and Robin seven they left the local school, where they were the only boys in their class, and started at the preparatory department of Porotora Royal School. This meant a daily journey of three miles each way across the town. So, for the next two years, as the boys cycled through, talking to one another at the tops of their voices, the whole of Enniskillen knew what they had been doing and what they planned.

After two years their time at Porotora came abruptly to an end. In the summer term of 1922 the most important and, at the time, the most tragic, event of Denis's young life took place. On the driveway leading to the school, during a fight between two rival groups of boys, he was blinded in the right eye as glass from his spectacles was shattered by a flying stone.

There followed an anxious six weeks in a Belfast hospital. Denis's mother stayed in the city and sat with him every day. After three operations it was decided to remove the eye. There was danger of infection spreading to the other eye, which would make him totally blind.

For Denis, at the age of eleven, the event did not seem as traumatic as it obviously was for his parents. He remembers best the working model steam-engine he was given by his father, as a consolation. But for Jim and Gwen Burkitt there was great fear, both during the early days and for the future. It was a time when they both leaned heavily on their Christian faith and the comfort of friends.

The loss of an eye was not in fact the serious handicap feared by Denis's parents. In his medical work Denis often proved capable of seeing with one eye what others before him had failed to see with two! From the time he left hospital, the possessor of a new glass eye, he determined not to let his handicap beat him.

Four years later, when the family moved to Laragh, he learned to shoot left-handed and it became a favourite winter sport for the two brothers to go hunting rabbits, woodcock and snipe on the bishop's neighbouring estate — with permission, of course.

In his father's eyes Denis could do no wrong. If anything was amiss, it was generally Robin who got the blame. The only misdemeanour Robin can remember, in which Denis shared his guilt, was when they chased the family cat through a large puddle in front of the house at Lawnakilla.

Denis may have been well-behaved — there is no evidence to the contrary. But he certainly was not a model pupil. True to the Burkitt tradition, he preferred always to do what he wanted, or (should we say) what he thought was right, rather than what was expected of him. He had little concern for his appearance: his tie was usually crooked and his hair went unbrushed.

At his studies Denis was, on his own admission, mediocre — right up to the end of his first year at Dublin University. At the time of his eye accident his reading ability was little above what was needed to enjoy a good comic. The only prize he remembers getting at school was for photography. This was his chief hobby from an early age at Lawnakilla, where he and Robin set up their first dark-room. As a research tool it was to be of greater value in later life than his scant knowledge of the classics.

After the accident, and largely because of it, his mother decided that the boys should go to boarding-school. She thought it would be an embarrassment both to the school and to the boys if they went back to Porotora after Denis left hospital. Father was not so sure. But, as is often the way with schooling, mother's wishes prevailed. In the autumn of that same year, they journeyed to Tre-Arddur Bay, near Holyhead in North Wales.

To Robin and Denis it was an alien land. Their clear Irish lilt, which in later years Robin lost more easily than Denis, set them apart. They looked forward eagerly to the end of each school term and to coming home. The boat left Holyhead at midnight and arrived at Greenore on the east coast of Ireland at eight in the morning.

The two boys were usually out of their bunks and up on deck before it got light, waiting for the first signs of the Mourne Mountains and the entrance to Carlingford Lough. And on the fifty-mile train journey across country to Enniskillen they peered eagerly through the carriage window and the smoke, until they could see their own 'mountains'; no more than hills in reality, but for them a sign that they were nearing home.

CHAPTER 2

A New Direction

Preparatory school at Tre-Arddur Bay, followed by secondary school at Dean Close in Cheltenham, occupied an uneventful seven years for Denis. No great ambition spurred him to academic achievement. It was assumed he would go on to university, and taken for granted it would be Trinity College, Dublin, where two uncles before him had graduated.

But what should he study? Apart from his better-forgotten experience of surgery at the hand of Uncle Roland, the only profession Denis knew at close quarters was his father's bridge- and road-building. He and Robin had already discussed and firmly rejected any idea of becoming doctors or dentists. Was the memory of a decade earlier still so vivid?

More to please his father than from any sense of vocation, Denis enrolled at Trinity's school of engineering. (A year later, Robin was to come up to study modern languages, with a view to joining the diplomatic service.) It was an unpromising freshman who travelled to Dublin in 1929, lacking in confidence, impaired in sight, poor both academically and at sport, and without any sense of vocation.

Fifty years later, Denis was made an honorary Fellow of Trinity, its highest award — for service, not to engineering, but to medicine and surgery. The important events responsible for this change of direction took place in his first year at university. They began during the second term, on a cross-country run.

Denis was not keen on running but he found it a good way of getting out into the fresh air. On one of the runs he was overtaken by a fellow student who, in conversation afterwards, invited him to 'Number 40'. This was the name given to a small group of undergraduates who met regularly for prayer and Bible study in Room 40 — a vacant room belonging to one of the Fellows of the college.

Denis had no misgivings about going along. But he was severely taken aback when, after a number of weeks, a much older student cornered him and challenged him with an embarrassing question. The gist of it was: had he ever responded to the claims that Jesus Christ, the Son of God, made on his life?

Since he had been brought up in a Christian home and confirmed with the rest of his age at school, Denis had come to assume that regular attendance at church, participation in communion and tolerably good behaviour, gave him, as he put it, 'an odds-on chance of a place in heaven'. But now it seemed his concept of the Christian life was wide of the mark. What was needed was a personal commitment.

This was Denis's first encounter with Christians who firmly believed that what really counted was not what *they* did, but what Christ had already done on their behalf through his death and resurrection. He had died for men and women as individuals, so they needed to respond as individuals. The faith of these Christians had an assurance Denis had not encountered before and he grasped it with enthusiasm. Looking back at this crucial event in later years, Denis realized the courage it took for one student to present such a challenge to another.

'Whether or not it was the right approach, I am profoundly grateful that God used this deeply-committed student to crystallize my faith. Then and there, with very little understanding of the implications for my future, I made up my mind to follow the calling of Christ and be identified in the college as a Christian.'

His new convictions at first made him rather intolerant of the views of others, even other Christian groups within the university. Along with his new friends from Room 40, he frowned on such 'worldly' activities as dancing, the cinema, theatre and card-playing. As his experience in the Christian faith grew, so his views of these activities mellowed. But he never regretted making such an open stand in those early days, either at the university or back home at Laragh.

Though quick to recount, these events — the invitation and challenge, and Denis's response — were vital in determining the new direction which his life was about to take. He now believed that God had a purpose for his life and became increasingly convinced it was not engineering. Just why he should have thought it was medicine is now a little unclear, even to him. It may have been the influence of a number of medical students among his new-found friends. Whatever the reason, before the end of his first year Denis felt convinced that medicine was to be his true vocation.

Just to be sure, he put God to the test, like the Old Testament hero, Gideon, with his fleece. Denis's 'fleece' was twenty scraps of paper shaken up in a cardboard box. If the only one with a big 'M' scribbled on it came out when he dipped in his hand, a medical career it would be.

That is exactly what happened. And on that flimsy basis the decision was made.

There were still two problems to overcome before Denis could enrol in the autumn at Trinity's medical school — chemistry and his father. He had done badly at chemistry during his first year as an engineering student. How could he be a doctor if he failed a subject as important as this, especially since it was part of the medical school entrance examination? Out went another 'fleece'.

'Dear God,' he prayed, 'if I am to be a doctor, please get me through my chemistry.'

The prayer, plus a lot of hard work during the summer vacation back home, seemed to do the trick. He came near to the top when he took the entrance exam.

With this success, the old Burkitt family quality of single-mindedness at last began to assert itself. Knowing the direction in which he was to go was all the incentive Denis needed to overcome any lack of intellectual ability. In later life he argued in public and in private that, for anyone to succeed in life, the right direction is everything. He often quotes John Oxenham's poem:

'One ship sails East and another West,
While the selfsame breezes blow;
It's the set of the sail and not the gale
That bids them where to go.
Like the waves of the sea
Are the storms of the fates,
As we journey along through life;
It's the set of the sail
That decides the goal,
And not the storms and strife.'

The one remaining hurdle to get over was his father. How would he react to his eldest son giving up his beloved engineering for medicine? Denis wondered how he would take it and he found it hard to pluck up courage to tell him. The first opportunity came one evening over supper, soon after he had arrived home for the summer vacation.

After several false starts, he blurted out, 'I want to give up engineering and become a doctor.'

There was silence. Attempts to explain his reasons went unheard. The mealtime was spoiled, as the rest of the family looked towards father. He got up from the table and sat instead in his armchair by the fireplace. Obviously he was not pleased. As a successful engineer, James Burkitt had taken great pride in the fact that his eldest son would follow in his footsteps. Denis also knew that the extra years at college would affect the family financially. These were the days before there were government grants for education.

But, if father was upset, mother could barely conceal her delight.

'My son, Doctor Burkitt,' she repeated quietly, with evident pride, as she cleared the table.

In fact it did not take long for father to get over his disappointment. He was too fond of Denis to let his own personal aspirations get in the way of his son's future. He could probably also see the change which had taken place in Denis and recognize the signs of Burkitt determination.

By the time Denis returned to Trinity in the autumn of 1930, as a first-year medical student, the transformation was complete. His course was set for a medical career and he attacked his work with new confidence and enthusiasm. He moved rooms to be with Robin, who came up to join him that year. For the next five years he remained at, or near, the top of his class, and during that time determined he would become a surgeon.

After graduating as a Bachelor of Medicine, Denis spent a further three-and-a-half years in post-graduate studies, working as a house surgeon in a number of hospitals throughout the country — Chester, Dublin, Preston and Poole among them. Life was busy. Out of working hours he helped to run ward services. He took part in open-air evangelistic meetings and made many new friends. He had his first taste of public speaking, which was to become almost a second career much later in his life.

Another lifelong habit, started during Denis's first year as a house surgeon, was keeping a diary. He did so intermittently at first, and always in an odd assortment of notebooks. These dated notes form a record of a spiritual pilgrimage, rather than of daily happenings. They are preoccupied with confessions, doubts, prayers and disappointments. Above all, the diaries record a concern for the spiritual lives of those doctors and nurses he worked with, and the patients he worked for. They reveal a man wanting to share his faith with others and to point out the priorities of life as he saw them.

On the wards, Denis gave away Christian literature and tracts much as the nurses dispensed pills — regularly and with the needs of the individual patient in mind. It was a practice that got him into trouble with his superiors early on, as this entry in his diary shows:

Wednesday 17 July 1935
Felt much responsibility. One of my male patients died. Was able to give away a few booklets.
Thursday 18 July
Gave a patient a book of Psalms and asked him to read 24 and 34. Also quoted Isaiah 4:13. He died next morning.
Friday 19 July
Mr Woodruffe (the consultant surgeon) told me it had come

back to him I was distributing religious tracts to patients. He forbade me to do so any longer. It may seem a big blow but God will work things all right. In the afternoon I read: 'Be not afraid but speak, and hold not thy peace. For I am with thee.' I have spoken to no one here about their souls yet.

He was not easily discouraged. Throughout his time as house surgeon he continued what he saw as an essential ministry to his patients, sometimes with results that were to test his faith.

Friday 23 July 1937
Last night we operated on a man whose abdomen was full of foul-smelling pus. Just closed it up with a tube. Mr Forrest told me straight, the patient would die. Told me to get a post-mortem ready, expecting his patient to be gone by the morning. As I read my *Daily Light* God gave me James 5:14–18: 'Is any sick among you? Let him call for the elders of the church; and let them pray over him . . . and the prayer of faith shall save the sick . . .' I took it as a promise for this man (aged 22) and prayed for his recovery. He got worse during the night. As I thought of his condition I couldn't see how he could recover, but I thought my God was omnipotent. This morning he was slightly better, and my faith was stronger. He has continued to improve ever since. Praise the Lord for his goodness.

Sunday 1 August
Took the service in the men's ward. Spoke to the man who had been healed in answer to prayer. He showed me a message scrawled on a bit of paper from a friend, telling him to look up to Jesus. So someone else must be praying for him too.

Thursday 5 August
Very disappointed. The man who had been so wonderfully healed died. I trust I may meet him in eternity. He was only in for two Sundays and hardly fit to listen. I thank God that on the one Sunday he was fit to listen I had the opportunity to show him the way to salvation.

Early on in his time as house surgeon, Denis had his first

chance to travel overseas — with a touch of adventure. During his first summer vacation after leaving Trinity, he and a friend interested in the work of the Spanish Gospel Mission set out on a camping holiday in Spain. They planned to follow in the footsteps of George Borrow, as recounted in his book *The Bible in Spain*, giving out tracts as he had done.

It was July 1936. A cargo boat from Liverpool carried them and their bicycles and tents to Bordeaux. They then travelled by train down to the border and spent their first night in Spain, in the small town of Irun, before going on to Bilbao. Their adventure had begun but it was not to last for long. Within a week the Spanish Civil War broke out and there were armed men fighting on the streets. The Basque region of northern Spain was not the place for peaceful foreigners to be camping out. As the two young men prepared nervously to bed down for another night in the shelter of a Bilbao sports stadium, the message came to them that other Britons were being evacuated from the area. A British destroyer would be leaving Santander within the next couple of days. They were advised to be on board. ·

So, sooner than they expected, they were back in Bordeaux, waiting for their cargo ship to take them home. It had been a short and cheap but adventurous holiday. Back home, Denis settled down again as house surgeon, moving eventually to Edinburgh, where he took and passed his examination for the Fellowship of the Royal College of Surgeons.

It was now the summer of 1938. The continuing Spanish Civil War and the rumblings of Hitler and Mussolini began to disturb the atmosphere at home. But for Denis, as a newly-qualified surgeon, the future looked good. He could look forward to a responsible hospital job, leading eventually to a secure consultancy post. That was not enough for him, however. Since God had so clearly led him into medicine and surgery, he knew he must seek divine guidance in the use of his growing skills.

He wanted to apply them where the need was greatest. And, with no shortage of surgeons at home, that meant overseas in some underdeveloped country. But where, and in what capacity? Should he be a missionary first, or a surgeon first? He needed time away from his hospital work to think.

Towards the end of 1938, he signed on as ship's surgeon on board the MV *Glen Shiel* of the Blue Funnel Line, for her voyage to Manchuria and back. The five-month round trip should give him all the thinking-time he needed. The pay was fair and the work minimal. He set sail on 14 November. For the first part of the voyage there were twelve passengers. The rest of the time it was just the captain and crew, largely Chinese. As the ship's surgeon, Denis was next in rank to the captain. Each morning the two would do the rounds together. For Denis, the rest of the day was usually free — to read, pray, think, talk to passengers and crew, or just do nothing.

They sailed through the Mediterranean, past Suez and the Malacca Straits, via Singapore, Hong Kong, Shanghai, up the coast of China to Manchuria and the port of Dairen. It was a rich experience. At each port Denis would go ashore, camera in hand, meeting with the local groups of Christians wherever possible.

On board the *Glen Shiel* he tried to tell the crew about his Saviour. His diary for the voyage makes very little reference to the places visited but is full of people's names, nationalities and conversations.

Denis's chief preoccupation during the voyage was to discover where God wanted him to spend his future. By the time the ship reached Shanghai on its return trip, it looked settled. He would be a surgeon first and missionary second, working possibly with the Colonial Service in West Africa. From port, he wrote home of his decision. And, two days after arriving back in London in March, he called at the Colonial Office to enquire about the Colonial Medical Service.

In the train, travelling north from London to Liverpool to take the ferry home to Ireland, he determined that when he did apply to the Colonial Office he would make it clear that he saw such service as a calling of God. When he finally applied, this uncompromising approach did not bring the response he was expecting.

CHAPTER 3

Call to Uganda

It was more than a year before Denis made his application to the Colonial Office. In the meantime, after a short period as locum following his return from Manchuria, he got a job as Resident Surgical Officer at the Prince of Wales Hospital in Plymouth. These were the days before Britain brought in a National Health Service, when senior surgeons often gave their services free and the more junior RSOs did all the emergency work.

On 3 September 1939, two months after Denis started at the Prince of Wales, war was declared on Germany. As a naval port, Plymouth became a dangerous place and soon there were servicemen among the hospital patients. At the end of his first six months' contract, Denis found it hard to decide whether to remain in Plymouth, or to seek further surgical training elsewhere.

Faced with important decisions like this, he was readily influenced by verses of Scripture. About this time he read in an Officers' Christian Union magazine the words of the angel to Joseph and Mary, after they had run away to Egypt with the young Jesus: 'Be there until I bring thee word.'

Choosing to ignore the dangers of taking an isolated verse out of context, Denis saw this as guidance. He reapplied for his RSO job at Plymouth and got it. That was a choice of momentous importance because, half-way through his second six months, Olive Rogers arrived from her home in Seaford to become a trainee nurse. She did not see herself as a latter-day Florence Nightingale, but there was a war on and nursing was a better choice at the age of nineteen than going into the forces.

There was no hint of a lifelong partnership in their first meeting — on the contrary. Olive had been given a vaccination that had gone septic. As the doctor on duty, Denis was called in by the sister-in-charge to give his advice, which was to stick a plaster on it! How casual, thought Olive, who was not much impressed, and even less so later, when she found she was allergic to plasters.

Their next meeting created a problem of a different kind for Olive. Coming from a Christian home, she wanted to find a place of worship in Plymouth on her free Sundays. A woman doctor at the hospital invited her along to the lively local Anglican church, St Andrew's, the next Sunday they were both off-duty.

They arranged to meet outside. Olive got there first and, when her friend arrived, she had brought Denis with her. It looked as if Olive was going to play gooseberry. She was not to know that Denis had numerous friends amongst the hospital staff, male and female.

After the service the woman doctor had to go to a branch hospital in another part of the city, leaving Denis to offer Olive a lift in his small car. Back at the hospital Olive went straight on duty, only to be summoned immediately to the sister's office. Sister made it clear that Olive would get nowhere in nursing if she carried on like that. Nurses, especially junior probationers, did not go out with doctors on the staff.

Two months later, Denis left Plymouth for a more responsible post up north in Barnsley. Olive expected never to see or hear from him again. And it came as a total surprise when, the following Christmas, almost six months later, she received a card followed by a letter.

What had prompted Denis to write? Was it his readings from the Old Testament love-poem, the Song of Solomon, which stirred thoughts of love? As he admits in his diary, the Song was certainly becoming a new book to him.

His diary at this time also reveals that his thoughts concerning a wife were closely interlinked with the continually recurring ideas about going overseas as a non-professional missionary.

18 January 1941
After lunch today I read the daily portion in *Springs in the Valley*. Here is part of the text. 'When we want to know God's will there are three things which will always concur: the inward impulse, the Word of God and the trend of circumstances. Never start until all three agree.' I feel that in my case the three lights are coming into line. Also I feel I ought to have a wife before going abroad, but God will undertake for this if I seek his kingdom first.

Shortly after Christmas, Denis at last decided the time was right to send his application to the Colonial Office, asking for a job in the Medical Service in West Africa. He made it quite clear that behind the application was a Christian conviction and desire to serve God amongst the underprivileged. The response should not have surprised him.

Friday 21 February
A big bomb fell today. I got a letter from the Colonial Office saying it could not consider my application on account of my having lost an eye. I was stunned but brought it all to God in prayer.

Bitterly disappointed and convinced it was his uncompromising stand, rather than impaired sight, which caused them to reject him, he took comfort from the belief that, when God wants to do something big, he starts with a difficulty as a test of faith — like the Red Sea which barred the way for the Israelites fleeing from Egypt.

Little did he know how big that something was going to be. But comfort in his disappointment was not long in coming.

Saturday 22 February
Two things have been sent to greatly console me today. I got a grand letter from Olive Rogers. And God spoke to me through 1 Kings 12, verse 24: 'Ye shall not . . . fight . . . what has happened I have caused to happen.'

By the following month Olive Rogers was being referred to in his diary simply as Olive.

'Looked for a letter from Olive, but again disappointed — "the trying of your faith worketh patience".'

When Olive did write, she got replies by return of post. Heavy bombing in Plymouth no doubt increased his anxiety, not without cause. Friends of his had already been injured and their homes bombed.

Although 300 miles away, Denis continued to have great concern for the work still going on at the Prince of Wales Hospital, in particular the ward services which he had been responsible for starting, soon after arriving at Plymouth, and which continued to be of great benefit to both patients and staff.

Depressed at his rejection by the Colonial Service, but still believing that his future was to be overseas, Denis was at first tempted to fight against the decision. After all, he had already proved his ability as a surgeon, despite having only one eye. And if the real reason for rejection was his Christian commitment, there were plenty of people in government service before him — doctors, vets, administrators and agriculturalists — who had been dedicated to such work because of their religious convictions.

But, as he explored other avenues within the Colonial Service, he was quickly discouraged by what he found.

'Learned that the Sudan Medical Service would not take people over thirty. This depressed me a little.' He was just thirty at the time. 'All vacancies filled for the Southern Rhodesian Medical Service.'

His frustration at being rejected and seeing no way ahead was making him restless. Within a few weeks he began thinking about resigning his position as RSO at Barnsley, of getting out of this 'surgical rut', perhaps even getting out of surgery altogether, to become a medical missionary.

He was pulled in one direction by a desire to be in Plymouth, where so many of his friends were having a hard time and where Olive was still training, and in the other direction by the persistent conviction that he should be working overseas in some deprived part of the world.

But, if he resigned from Barnsley and did not want another RSO post and could not get into the Colonial Service, what was he to do? Well, there was a war on. He reasoned that perhaps this could be his non-professional missionary work for the time being. It was not a decision to be taken lightly but the arguments he was able to put down on paper in favour of taking such a step seemed to be overwhelming.

1. Men are needed badly.
2. I have no ties and therefore ought to go before those with ties.
3. I don't feel I should do more hospital jobs, in which case I would be automatically recruited.
4. There is need for Christian testimony in the army.
5. It will teach me much and be good training, no matter what kind of work I have to do.

In his own mind, one obstacle in the way of leaving Barnsley was having no one to carry on organizing the ward services which he had started there too, and to which he felt so committed. This problem was overcome with the arrival of a new casualty officer, willing to take on the spare-time task. So, considering the facts, there seemed no alternative. Into the army he would go.

Within three months of his rejection by the Colonial Service he had applied for a commission, passed his medical in York, resigned from Barnsley, and was on his way, at the end of a very hot June, to the Royal Army Medical Corps Training Depot in Hampshire.

From there he was posted as an army surgeon to the 219 Field Ambulance Unit at Witton, outside Norwich. He had no surgical responsibilities but learned to be an officer.

For the next year or so, life for Lieutenant (later Captain) Burkitt MB, FRCS was routine — route marches, clinics, leave, taking services and Bible studies, the occasional locum in civvy street, and more route marches. During this time, Olive and Denis corresponded regularly and met whenever he had a few days' leave and could get down to Plymouth. They picnicked, and talked and sunbathed together.

It was not until November 1942 that the pace of their friendship quickened. It began with a 'memorable' weekend when Denis travelled down to Plymouth in the early morning on a forty-eight-hour pass. After breakfasting at the home of a friend, they walked and talked. Next day, Olive's mother and brother also came down to visit. Denis was surprised just how much they knew about him.

Before parting with their first-ever kiss at the railway station, the young couple walked arm-in-arm along the Hoe — 'it being a beautiful starry night'.

Towards the end of February 1943 Denis again had forty-eight-hours' leave and he asked Olive to join him in London. She travelled up from Plymouth overnight and arrived at Paddington station at 7.30 a.m., tired and dishevelled. Denis proposed to her, there and then.

After breakfast at the station hotel they walked in St James's Park, waiting for Mappin and Webb to open, to buy the ring. It was the natural outcome of months of a gradually deepening relationship.

Denis had found his 'ideal' partner, one who shared the same Christian convictions and was prepared to put them above everything else. She had once written to him saying that 'friendship must be based on a mutual love for Jesus'. For her part, Olive had no illusions about Denis's unwillingness to compromise. She remembered too well the reprimanding letter she received for wanting to take part in Sunday rehearsals for the hospital's Christmas concert.

Being married to him was not going to be easy. It would probably mean living abroad, possibly as a missionary's wife. He had made that clear. But he had not warned her that it might mean long periods of separation, or just how soon after marriage that separation would come. He had not realized that himself. But soon after they became engaged there was talk of his field ambulance being sent overseas. It gave him the opportunity to get Olive to agree to a wedding date.

Olive was not so sure. She was in her last year of training and due to take her finals soon. Once married she would not want to continue working at Plymouth, where they were both so well known. But she had promised the matron she would stay for another year after qualifying. Denis's argument, however, proved very persuasive. She agreed to risk matron's wrath by marrying him in July, if she passed her exams in June.

They were married on a forty-eight-hour pass on 28 July at Seaford Parish Church and started their honeymoon strap-hanging on a bus, which left them three miles to walk to their hotel and a cold supper. Next day, they took photos, picked wild flowers, cut a walking-stick from a Sussex hedge and read together from Henry Drummond's book about Christian love, *The Greatest Thing in the World*.

Travel restrictions had made it impossible for Denis's relatives to get over from Enniskillen for the wedding. So it was not until two months later, when the newly-weds journeyed to Ireland to explore Denis's childhood haunts, that his parents saw Olive for the first time. On the very first morning of the holiday Denis received his overseas posting orders. It became an embarkation leave and the prelude to two-and-a-half years of separation.

Back in England, Olive went home to Reading while Denis collected his pith helmet. As she prepared to take up a nursing job in Eastbourne, Denis set sail from Glasgow, for some tropical destination unknown. Spain, the Mediterranean, Port Said — a familiar route to him — were followed by a dusty Suez transit camp, where he needed a stout mat to kneel on for his night-time prayer in his tent.

The troop-ship finally docked at Mombasa. He was in Africa. Not West Africa, where he had wanted to serve when he had applied to the Colonial Office. This was East Africa, where his Uncle Roland had once put the fear of God into his Nairobi patients, and where Denis himself was one day to begin his medical safari.

No sooner had they docked than he was on his way north-west by train to Nairobi, where he spent two weeks before being posted to a military hospital in Mombasa. There was just time to visit Uncle Roland's old rooms and the Brethren Memorial Hall, which had grown out of the informal prayer meetings and Bible studies he had started a quarter of a century before.

During the next eighteen months, Denis's work as an army surgeon enabled him to see a great deal of East Africa — by ambulance train, from the air and over rough and dusty roads. He learned Swahili, the most widely-used language in East Africa, and he attended native services in Mombasa Cathedral. He made new friends, African as well as European. He read Olive's many letters from home and started Bible studies and services for the men and officers.

In March 1944 he flew 600 miles north into Somalia, to the heat, glare and worldliness of Mogadishu. It proved a time of spiritual loneliness, a wilderness time in every sense. He had little work. He lost his monthly field allowance. And his kitbag containing his few belongings, which was supposed to come up on the next convoy, never did arrive. He gave up hope of promotion, or of 'leaving this place in under a year'.

Against this background of desolation Denis learned much, about himself and about the Somali Africans. His Bible was his greatest comfort.

'In my darkest moments Job was a great help to me. I complained, inwardly at least, about this desolation, this barren country and yet I had said and sung that I was willing to go wherever God sent me. How easy to say and really not mean. Before these troubles lifted, relative contentment came, largely through the Word. For all this I am grateful, though repentant that I so badly stood the test.'

On 14 June, after three months and many false starts, he eventually got away from Mogadishu by road convoy. His kitbag finally caught up with him in Nairobi.

It was not all wilderness. Back in Kenya, as surgeon-in-charge at a station hospital in the Kenyan Highlands and finally promoted to major, Denis found the dust and the glare replaced by 'sparkling bright specks of sand, everywhere reflecting the sun's rays'. He continued to make new friends and with one of these, another Christian officer, Norman Miller, he spent the only long holiday he had while in Africa. Together they enjoyed six weeks of intensive travel through the Ugandan countryside, visiting mission stations, getting a first-hand picture of what life in the country was like.

This was his first visit to the country where he and Olive would raise their family. Here he would discover the cause of Burkitt's lymphoma and lay the foundations for his dietary theories. And here, in 1962, he would take part in the Independence celebrations that preceded Uganda's sad decline and destruction under the tyranny of Idi Amin, ten years later.

Denis somehow knew that this holiday was a turning-point in his life. He had been challenged by the country and its people, particularly the Ugandan Christians he met. He wrote of his experience to Olive in persuasive terms. In her replies she at last seemed resigned to joining him in Africa, if he got his release from the army. Believing that the war was coming to an end, he had already sent off his second application to the Colonial Office, this time specifically for Uganda. Surely he would not be rejected on medical grounds a second time?

CHAPTER 4

Lango: Early Detection

As Olive worked on the wards in Eastbourne, she sometimes paused to look at her wedding ring. Was she really married? Like so many other wartime newly-weds, she found it hard to be separated for so long, after just a few weeks as a wife. Not only was she in a different country from Denis. They were in different wars. For Denis it was a war of adventure and travel, as an army officer and surgeon. Olive's was a war of civilian casualties — and doodle-bugs crossing the coast at night.

The life in Africa which Denis described in his frequent letters was hard for her to imagine. Still harder was the idea of being a bush doctor's wife. Unlike Denis, she felt no missionary calling. Just a few months before Denis's decisive holiday in Uganda, Olive had written to him: 'Darling, do you really want to make your home abroad?'

The letter caused him much pain and drove him to pray that God might 'make her ready'. Through prayer, and Denis's persuasive pen, Olive had come round to his way of thinking by the time the Colonial Office acknowledged his application form.

But the waiting was not yet over. Although there was talk of peace, the war went on. Denis received instructions to prepare for posting to Burma, where the East African troops were still engaged in jungle warfare against the Japanese. After some training at the Royal Army Medical Corps Depot in Nairobi, he marched to Nairobi station at the head of a contingent of several hundred men. It was his thirty-third birthday.

After a few days in transit camp on the beach at Mombasa, he and the rest of the contingent embarked, as they believed, for the battlefields of Burma. But the war situation changed. Extra surgeons were no longer needed in Burma. Denis and his medical companions were landed at Colombo, in Sri Lanka (then Ceylon).

There was a short period in a jungle camp and then he was posted as surgeon to an Indian military hospital. He remained in Ceylon for the next year, serving in three different military hospitals, before receiving a posting to Bangkok. But then the Japanese surrendered and, on his way by ship, he learned that he was not now needed in Thailand. Instead he was disembarked at Singapore. From there, by many stages, he was flown back to England and Olive.

It was almost eighteen months from the time he left Africa to the time he arrived back in England, with the war finally at an end. Husband and wife were reunited in Eastbourne and then went on to Ireland for his demobilization and a new life together — for a while.

Within a month of Denis's return, Olive was pregnant and he had been interviewed by the Colonial Office in London for a post in Uganda. In the six weeks between the interview and getting the letter of acceptance Denis became very depressed. Olive was unwell and having doubts again. She had discovered that there would be another period of separation, while Denis set up home for them in a disrupted post-war Uganda.

And the prospect of becoming a father had turned Denis's thoughts to the domestic problems of raising and educating a family. How much easier it would be if he took a consultant's position in England.

As it was, it looked as if he might have to give up all idea of being a surgeon — the very job he wanted most of all — if he went to Uganda. During his interview at the Colonial Office he was asked whether he was willing to work in any medical capacity. The temptation was to stipulate surgery but he realized that to lay down any conditions would be contrary to his sense of calling. Instead he promised to do his best in whatever sphere of work was given him, adding with emphasis that his experience so far had been almost exclusively surgical.

Great relief and peace of mind came with the letter saying he had been accepted for the post of medical officer in Uganda. His path ahead was finally decided. Things were also made easier when, a few days later, Olive came to him in their home at Laragh. She had been reading his African diaries, where he had expressed concern about her doubts and fears. Frank discussion brought them to their knees together and there was a new bond of unity.

The same day, Denis heard that the MD thesis he had prepared in slack moments in the Far East and submitted to Dublin University had been accepted.

While waiting for his sailing-date, Denis kept busy as a locum for a general practitioner in Fivemiletown, fifteen miles from Laragh. He also took a course in midwifery — he wanted to be prepared for anything in his work amongst the native Africans. In fact the only babies he was ever required to deliver in Africa were by Caesarean section.

The rest of the waiting-time was spent with Olive, filling crates and boxes with their few belongings and many books, along with all the things they imagined they would not be able to get once they reached their destination.

Getting the crates to Enniskillen station proved a more formidable task than had been expected. The family car was not big enough. It required the use of the neighbour's cart, drawn by his donkey, Jerusalem. The five-mile journey normally took two hours but it was two days before anyone could catch the donkey — a common cause of procrastination in Ireland in those days.

The delay was fortuitous. Just before the donkey set off for the station, the postman arrived. The letter he handed to Denis detailed a change of address for his luggage not-wanted-on-voyage. Two days earlier and it would have gone to the wrong baggage handlers in Southampton.

Even more memorable was the day in September when Denis left for Uganda. As he and Olive knelt by their Victorian bed, they fought back the tears. How long would they be separated?

Olive's pregnancy and their closeness over the past seven months made it an even more painful day than the parting three years earlier.

It was a comfort to Denis to discover, on reaching London from Ireland, that Olive could join him, either at the end of the month, or as soon as the baby was born. They chose the latter, because plans for the baby had already been made. So it was six months before they met again, time for Denis to get settled in and prepare a home for Olive and their baby.

Baby Judith was born on a cold day at the end of December, into the warmth and love of the Laragh home. Within two months she was sailing south with her mother on their maiden voyage to a sunnier land — Africa. Their ship, the *Winchester Castle*, had been used as a troop-carrier and was still in wartime camouflage. On this voyage it carried twice the normal load of people. Many, like Olive, were travelling with their children to be reunited with husbands. Some were going as far as South Africa.

All the way to Mombasa Olive and Judith shared a cabin with eleven other people — five mothers and six children. The bunks were small and there was little room to move. Judith's carrycot rested on an iron table strapped to Olive's bunk. Nappies were strung along the corridors and lined the bathrooms.

Olive later recalled that it was a grim voyage. Every sort of disease broke out during the three weeks they were at sea. The hospital was full. Children with measles were confined to their cabins. Olive felt sure her baby would die before seeing her father. 'Thank God,' she cried, when she saw Denis waiting at the Mombasa quayside, as the boat docked.

Just to be reunited was bliss. And for Denis the first sight of his new daughter was in itself worth the 750-mile journey by truck and train from Lira, administrative centre of the up-country district of Lango, where Denis had been posted on his arrival six months earlier. The three spent two nights in a small hotel in Mombasa before beginning the long journey by train to the Kenya–Uganda border.

As Olive travelled on, her feelings were a mixture of excitement at the prospect of setting up a home of her own at last, and apprehension at learning to live, as she thought, 'in the jungle'. They arrived at the border town of Tororo at six in the morning. She could not believe her eyes. There was dew on the grass, roses by the station, and the sweetest of smells in the air. She was overwhelmed by the surrounding beauty.

In post-war Uganda cars were hard to come by. When he had first arrived, Denis used a puncture-prone bike to get around the station and an ambulance to reach the outposts of his district. But now he had acquired a Ford pick-up for £140. In this Olive and Judith began their first journey into the heart of Uganda. Holes in the floor-boards conspired with water in the pot-holed dirt roads to ensure that Olive arrived with her legs caked red with mud.

Their new home in Lira was a square, colonial-style bungalow with a veranda surrounding it and a red corrugated roof on top. Arriving from war-torn Britain, where everyone was so busy, Olive was taken aback by the number of servants Denis employed. She teased him for his softness, as he explained that he had a good salary by African standards and men were pleading for work.

On £600 a year he could afford to pay his head boy Yusufu £18 and the part-time gardener £6 a year. But there was also a cook and his helper, as well as a boy to help Yusufu. And, as if that was not enough, Denis had taken on an ayah to help Olive look after the baby. Olive did not mind someone else washing the nappies but she was quite determined to look after Judith herself. Yusufu stayed with the Burkitts as a loved member of the family until they left Africa in 1966.

In the house, the toilet was a bucket under a wooden seat and was emptied daily into an ox-drawn cart. A wood fire under a corrugated iron tank gave hot water in the evenings, piped directly to a bath. Cooking was done in a separate building, blackened by years of smoke from a wood-stove.

Uganda was a stable country in 1947. As a British Protectorate it had a governor, a British-style judiciary system with judges and magistrates, and experts in medicine, agriculture, animal welfare and forestry. A district commissioner was in

charge of each of the country's dozen or so districts, of which
Lango was one.

During the eighteen months Denis was stationed in the
district capital, Lira, he was responsible as the district medical
officer for the health care of 250,000 people, living in a
7,000-square-mile area. This included responsibility for a
100-bed hospital and its staff. He was assisted by a locally
qualified African doctor who was later to become leader of one
of the country's political parties and a cabinet minister for a
while, following the downfall of Idi Amin.

Facilities within the hospital were limited. Surgical instru-
ments were sterilized over a primus stove. One room, which
had been an office, served as operating-theatre, sterilizing-
room, cleaning-room, washing-room and anaesthetic-room.
The anaesthetic was sometimes open ether, given by a local
man with no nursing experience. Or Denis would himself
inject into the spinal canal to numb the patient's body from
the waist down for two hours, without further help from the
assistant.

On the rare occasions when emergency operations were done
at night, an oil pressure-lamp from home was hung over the
table. There was endless scope for improvisation. For Denis,
who hated wasting money, this was great fun. Gloves punc-
tured during operations were mended just like bicycle tubes,
using even older gloves for patching. Despite the primitive
conditions, the people of Lira were better served then than they
would be some thirty years later when, under Amin, surgeons
would operate without gloves or soap.

Most of the Europeans living in Uganda were there for the
benefit of the Ugandan people. They were either government
officials or missionaries. Few were settlers, as they were in
Kenya. In the Lira area there were a dozen or so white people
with whom the Burkitts mixed on social occasions. There was a
good deal of sport — particularly tennis, which they both loved
— which was just as well, since the other main leisure activity
was propping up the bar. Denis had strong views about that.

While he was in the army, Denis's teetotal views were
accepted without question by his fellow officers. In Lira it was

not so easy. During the six months he spent alone, preparing for Olive to arrive, he kept no alcohol in the house. When she arrived and began turning the house into a home, putting up curtains and arranging flowers, they also began to entertain. That, at the very least, meant offering a sherry before dinner.

Making people feel at home, without compromising their own principles, often meant that Olive and Denis spent far more on food than it would have cost them in organizing sundowners. But from the start Denis was conscious that, in a country where the British residents numbered less than one tenth of one per cent, each one should set an example.

The discovery that African doctors tended either to drink to excess, or not to drink at all, strengthened his resolve. Among his saddest experiences was to watch the careers of good African doctors ruined because of their compulsion for the bottle. Surrounded by such casualties Denis had no qualms about siding with the abstainers.

The government hospital at Lira served the entire Lango district, which was inhabited largely by the Langi tribe. There were also twelve dispensaries in the outlying areas of the district, where an African with some medical training held a daily surgery. Once a week, Denis would visit two or three of these in turn, dispensing drugs and running a clinic. Taking his truck enabled him to ferry patients between the dispensaries and the hospital.

Sometimes Olive would go with him and they slept at night in some thatched or tin-roofed government rest-house. Despite the mosquitos, she enjoyed these excursions into the bush country around Lira. They went regularly to Boro-boro, where there was an Anglican mission station. Here Judith had been christened within two weeks of her arrival in Uganda.

An early pleasure for Olive was to be invited with Denis to the home of his African friends and colleagues for dinner. It was common for Europeans to invite their African friends and colleagues to their homes, but not so usual the other way round. For Olive this acceptance was all the more important, once she discovered that, after the district commissioner's wife, she ranked as the most senior woman on the station.

In these small ways Olive was eased into colonial life. At the same time Denis was being eased into what was to become his most important work while in Africa — geographical pathology, or the study of the effect of climate and geography on disease distribution.

Although officially a medical officer with responsibility for the general public health of the district, including schools, as well as the control of sleeping sickness and malaria, Denis quickly found that the most immediate good to the greatest number of people could be achieved by surgery. By the time he left Lira, after eighteen months, he had increased the annual number of major operations twentyfold, to more than 600.

The outstanding surgical problem he had to face was hydrocele — an abnormal build-up of fluid in the sac around a testicle. These swellings reached a far greater size than he had ever seen in Europe. The surgical cure was simple but some of the observations Denis was able to make were of great importance.

He noticed that most of his patients with hydrocele came from the eastern part of the district. Few were from the west. During visits to his outpost dispensaries he began to examine men for the disease. Warned in advance of the district medical officer's coming, the head man of the village would have fifty or more males lined up, ready to drop their shorts or trousers when he arrived.

From his findings he constructed a map of the district which showed a geographical distribution that ranged from thirty per cent of the male population suffering from hydrocele in the east down to around one per cent in the west. The cause of the disease was subsequently found to be a microscopic worm, transmitted by mosquito.

This small study of geographical distribution became the subject of one of the first of over 300 scientific papers written and published by Denis Burkitt dealing with many different diseases and was the first of many papers dealing with the

geography of disease. This one was published in the medical
journal *The Lancet*, but it had its first airing in Kampala, when
he presented it at a Uganda Medical Association meeting in
commemoration of the fiftieth anniversary of the arrival of Sir
Albert Cook in Uganda. This was the man who, in 1897, had
founded the Mengo Mission Hospital, which still stood on the
outskirts of Uganda's capital, Kampala. From it had grown
the nearby Mulago Hospital which had become the centre of
the Uganda government hospital system.

It was to Mulago Hospital that Denis was transferred after
eighteen months at Lira. For the first time he was officially
recognized as a surgeon. He was in fact one of only two
genuinely qualified surgeons in the country at that time. The
other, Professor Ian McAdam, had for some time been left
alone to do all the surgery at Mulago, with the result that he
himself developed a duodenal ulcer. Denis was asked to come to
his rescue.

From the time when it was intimated by the director of
medical services in Entebbe, the administrative capital, that
Denis might be moved to Mulago, to that of the actual move,
three months later, Denis went through the by now customary
period of misgivings and spiritual doubt. This time he was
concerned in case he did not get the job, knowing that it offered
him the chance to do what he was best qualified for.

As his diary shows, it was a time when he felt that his natural
ambition was in danger of conflicting with his desire to serve
God where he wanted.

Friday 5 December 1947
I have long been anxious about going to Kampala. Perhaps the
delay is due to my inward unwillingness to go or stay as God
wishes. I argue that my talents would be better served there, but
who made me a surgeon? God. Who gave me a Fellowship (of
the Royal College of Surgeons)? Who called me to Africa? Have
I not sung: 'Where he leads me I will follow'? Have I not a
thousand times prayed, 'Thy will be done'? May God have us
where he wants us.

It became clear that both God and the Colonial Office wanted Denis and his family in Kampala. Just a few days after Christmas and Judith's first birthday, they moved into their new home.

CHAPTER 5

Cancer Discovery

After a wartime lull, the hospital at Mulago had begun to expand again by the time Denis started working there. Expansion was largely a matter of adding another hut to the single-storey cluster which surrounded the main pavilion, a two-storey building further up the hill than most of the others. Already there were separate departments for surgery, medicine and gynaecology.

Although he had enjoyed the variety of work at Lira, Denis was glad of the opportunity which Mulago gave him to concentrate on surgery. It was, after all, what he was best at doing — even though, as he soon discovered from the example set by his new colleague, Professor Ian McAdam, there was still much room for improvement.

He also took satisfaction from the fact that East Africa's first mission hospital, Mengo, still stood nearby. It was back in 1896 that twelve missionaries sent out from England by the Church Missionary Society and led by Albert Cook had marched the 700 miles from Mombasa through forest, swamp, desert and mountain to reach the part of Uganda where Denis was now working.

The incentive to improve his surgical skills, and the needs of the many Ugandans who crowded every day to the hospital, left little time to think why the diseases that he knew to be common back home in Britain were so rare in Africa.

There was, however, one group of surgical problems to which he gave extra thought. Much of his work during the day was spent in orthopaedic surgery and, within months of arriving at Mulago, he developed a deep concern for the many Africans whose ulcerated or deformed legs he was having to amputate.

Amputation in Uganda left the victim immobile. There were no artificial limbs available. And, with only one leg, the amputee was often reduced to dependence on relatives, or to begging. Denis was determined to find a remedy for this problem.

That chance came during his first leave, after three years in Africa. By this time Denis's and Olive's second daughter, Carolyn, had been born. Back home, from August 1949 to April 1950 was a hectic eight months — at Laragh, where they spent Christmas together for the first time as a complete family, on the Isle of Wight, where Olive's parents now lived, at the new Staines home of brother Robin and his wife Vi, and in London, where Judith had to undergo an operation in Great Ormond Street Hospital.

Amidst all the rush, Denis found time to take part in a five-month post-graduate course in orthopaedic surgery at the National Orthopaedic Hospital. Here he saw how inexpensive artificial legs could be made from plastic materials, newly-developed for aircraft construction.

The resultant legs were not attractive to look at. They were intended as only temporary support, while the patient waited for a more permanent fitting. But, with a keen eye to doing things at minimal cost, Denis saw how, for just a couple of pounds, these legs could provide a longer-term answer to the needs of his crippled Africans.

On returning to Kampala he raised enough money to set up a small workshop. Here a promising school-leaver was put to work making legs from malleable plastic. The workshop was a big success. Eventually it was taken over by a full-time orthopaedic surgeon and it grew to become a training centre for surgical staff from all over Africa, wanting to learn how to make artificial legs that could bring freedom and mobility.

The work did not stop at providing limbs. A common sight around Kampala were the many sufferers from poliomyelitis, who sat helpless on the pavements, their legs too bent to walk.

It was a simple operation to straighten the legs but they were still weak and needed the support of callipers, which again cost money.

Or perhaps it required just a little imagination! For next to nothing Denis was able to get from the Kampala public works department lengths of iron rod used in making reinforced concrete structures for bridges and buildings. With these he made callipers attached to shoes that were open-toed, to allow for growth. The callipers were not adjustable. That would have cost too much. Instead, when a child outgrew his calliper it would be hung on a hook on the workshop wall and the next size taken down.

Next came crutches. Cheap African versions were available but they fitted uncomfortably under the armpit at one end and tended to dig into the ground at the other. By bending an iron rod to form a U-shape, Denis found he could make a comfortable crutch that rocked nicely on the ground. A length of broom handle fitted across the tops of the rod ends to form an arm-rest. Another length further down made a hand-grip. A crutch of this kind could be bent around the branch of a tree, and a hot poker used to drill the holes needed for the grip and arm-rest.

Denis enjoyed orthopaedic surgery. From his early days at Mulago he took a special interest in congenital deformities. He amassed a large collection of photographs of the many children born with deformed limbs. He might well have taken a full-time interest in this work if it had not been for an event so trivial at the time that he cannot remember exactly when it took place — except that it was early in 1957.

By that time he had been in Africa for ten years. He and Olive now had three daughters — Judith, Carolyn (called Cass, an abbreviation of the name her African nurse had given her) and Rachel. The hospital facilities had expanded considerably, to include three surgical units. Denis headed one. The other two were run by Ian McAdam, and by John Croot, who had arrived at Mulago Hospital as professor of surgery just two years after Denis. They were to become the only active surgeons ever knighted for their work in Africa.

The medical work had its own facilities and wards. The senior consultant physician on the medical side was Dr Hugh Trowell, subsequently described by Denis as the best-known physician of the time in East Africa. As fellow Christians Denis and Hugh, who later became an ordained Church of England vicar with a parish in Wiltshire, were friends even before Denis moved from Lira to Mulago.

They had first met in 1947, on that train in which Denis had travelled down to Mombasa to meet Olive from England. Hugh was travelling in style, requested by the East Africa Railway Company to look into the health and diet of railway workers, who were becoming increasingly restless over their wretched living conditions.

Hugh was something of an expert in nutrition, having been a pioneer in the recognition and treatment of kwashiorkor, before coming to Mulago from Kenya with his artist wife Margaret in 1935. At that time the mud floors and grass roofs of the collection of huts that formed Mulago Hospital were just being replaced by concrete and corrugated iron.

(Described by the World Health Organization as 'the most widespread and severe nutritional disorder known to medical science', kwashiorkor is caused by protein and calorie deficiency. Hugh Trowell discovered a remedy in fat-free milk.)

This 'best-known physician in East Africa' became a central character in the Burkitt story on that anonymous day in 1957. The Burkitts were due for their fourth leave in Britain. At the end of the morning's ward round at Mulago, Denis the surgeon was asked by Hugh the physician for his opinion about a young boy in the children's ward, where they both had patients.

The pathetic face of the five-year-old child was deformed by swellings on both sides of his upper and lower jaws. Both Denis and Hugh had seen single swellings before. These were cancerous tumours which had to be removed by disfiguring surgery. Left untreated, the tumours could double in size every forty-eight hours, and after a month or two death was inevitable.

But what Denis saw that day puzzled him. He had never seen

four swellings so equally spaced around a face before — not even in the textbooks. Could all four be caused by cancer? He examined the nervous child thoroughly. He made notes and, as was always his practice with any unusual sight, he took photographs. He could be sure of only one thing. Since surgery was out of the question, the little boy was going to die.

Denis might have dismissed the event as a tragic curiosity, had he not been at the District Hospital of Jinja a few weeks later. Jinja is at the head of the River Nile and some fifty miles east of Kampala. He was on a routine teaching round. As he talked to his students, something he caught sight of through an open window distracted his attention. A swollen-faced girl was sitting on the grass in the hospital grounds with her mother.

The surgeon's tour came abruptly to an end. He went in search of the unfortunate girl and found a case identical to the one he had seen recently at Mulago Hospital. Was this a coincidence, or were such disfigurements more common than he had supposed? He needed to know more. The bewildered child was driven with her mother the fifty miles back to Mulago, where she was photographed and examined. Then, helplessly, they watched her die.

Two such tragedies in so short a time demanded to be investigated. In his mind, Denis began linking them with the several single tumours he had seen and operated on. The singleminded determination, so characteristic of earlier Burkitts, began quietly to take hold. He had many other duties to perform but, over the next ten years, finding the cause and a solution to these deforming growths was to become an overriding passion.

One important result of examining the little girl before she died was the discovery of tumours in other parts of her body. This led Denis to search through past clinical records and autopsy reports at Mulago Hospital. Invariably, where there were jaw tumours, growths in other parts of the body were also found. He began keeping detailed records of patients sent to him by other doctors and from other hospitals in Uganda.

Increasingly he was convinced that there was a connection between the various tumours. Could there in fact be a common cause? One way of finding out was to study the age distribution of the recorded tumours. He knew that different forms of cancer had different age patterns. He found that the tumours were virtually unknown in children under two. They reached a peak between six and eight years and faded away in adolescence.

The rarity of the tumours below the age of two suggested that this was different from any previously-known form of cancer in children. And the consistency of age distribution confirmed, in Denis's mind at least, that there was a common cause. He sought the advice of pathologists at the adjacent Makerere College Medical School (of which Mulago was the teaching hospital). They were not sure. All their experience pointed to the belief that tumours developing in specific organs had their own specific causes.

Two of them, Professor Jack Davies and Dr Greg O'Conor, examined all 106 pathological slides in their collection of children's cancers that were similar to Denis's tumours. To their surprise, the tumours removed from the jaw were found to be indistinguishable under the microscope from those in other parts of the body. They were looking at a hitherto unrecognized form of lymphoma or lymph-tissue cancer. Denis had been right in coming to the conclusion, clinically, that tumours in different structures and organs were all the same type of cancer.

These discoveries meant that this one lymphoma (later given the name 'Burkitt's lymphoma') could be responsible for 50 per cent of all the cancer in children in tropical Africa, making it the commonest of all childhood cancers. Certainly it accounted for almost half the children's tumours recorded in the Kampala Cancer Registry.

Was this, then, a new form of cancer which, although now common, had not been recognized? Denis brushed up his schoolboy French, so that he could study the literature of West as well as East and Central Africa. Records of jaw tumours were rare. But he found them, along with tumours in other parts of the body. It was as though workers had observed and studied the individual trees but it was left to the special insight of this man to consider the forest for the first time.

He now wanted to know how far back records of the tumour went. What better place to start looking than in the historic Mengo Hospital? He scoured the notes of its founder, Albert Cook. He was rewarded by pictures and descriptions of growths dating back to the turn of the century. There was specific reference to tumours in the jaw, which Cook had simply called sarcomas — the name given to certain types of tumour — without identifying the category. Here was proof that Denis Burkitt was *not* dealing with a new disease.

A closer look at his own statistics revealed another remarkable factor. Patients with tumours came more frequently from the north and east of Uganda than from the south and west. His mind went back to the similar findings he had made at Lira, when he was studying the distribution of hydrocele. His encounter with geographical pathology was about to be renewed.

A catalyst in this was another Christian, Dr George Oéttle. Oéttle was ten years younger than Denis and a brilliant pathologist, specializing in cancer research. At the time of their meeting, at the end of 1957 in Kampala, he was director of the Cancer Research Unit of the South African Institute for Medical Research in Johannesburg, where he worked on many of the common African malignancies.

Denis introduced George Oéttle to some of his Mulago children who were suffering from jaw tumours. He showed him pictures and slides and explained his concern. Oéttle's response was categorical and authoritative. No such tumours occurred in South Africa. Denis knew that he had been given a vital clue. If it did not occur in South Africa, at what point between there and Mulago did it stop? Suddenly he felt sure that a study of the tumour's geographical distribution would prove the best way of arriving at its cause.

The appalling disfigurement caused by the jaw tumours had at least one benefit for researchers: it was very visible and readily diagnosed. Unlike internal tumours, it could not pass unnoticed by anyone looking for it. Denis selected the best of his many photographs and had a thousand leaflets printed, with pictures of various forms of facial tumour and a brief description of how tumours in other parts of the body could be detected.

Slowly he built up a mailing-list of government and mission hospitals throughout Africa. Leaflets were then sent, a few at a time, to the hundreds of doctors working in them. They were also handed out at conferences and to any visitors who came to Mulago. With each leaflet went a questionnaire, asking if tumours had been seen, and a note encouraging doctors to look out for signs they might previously have overlooked.

To finance this original approach to cancer research Denis applied for two government grants, worth £10 and £15, to cover printing and posting the leaflets. There can be few serious research projects which have been funded for less, and none that have had such a far-reaching influence on cancer research.

Over the next eighteen months he received replies from several hundred hospitals all over Africa. They came both from those who had seen the tumour and from those who had not. Answers to the questionnaire confirmed Denis's own findings that where there were jaw tumours there were also tumours in other parts of the body.

On the wall behind his office desk, Denis hung three maps: of Uganda, East Africa and the whole African continent. Using pins with home-made coloured heads (again to save money!) he plotted the results as they came in. Gradually a pattern emerged. It showed a band across tropical Africa, running between about ten degrees north and ten degrees south of the equator, where the tumours could be found. It also included a tail running down the east coast to the Natal/Mozambique border.

Here was the confirmation he needed that his lymphoma could be located geographically — across five million square miles of what was to become known as the lymphoma belt.

It was an exciting discovery that Denis wanted to share. He announced his initial findings to the hospital staff at one of their regular Saturday morning meetings. They were received with mild interest. Next he prepared a paper outlining the evidence for a lymphoma belt and presented it at the 1958 Annual

Meeting of the East African Association of Surgeons in Kampala in February.

Towards the end of the year, his first paper was published in the *British Journal of Surgery*. It aroused zero interest; not surprisingly perhaps, since it contained no hint of a cure for the terrible deformities it described. And why should readers in a developed country attach importance to the work of an unknown surgeon in a hospital hidden in Africa, concerning a disease which was exceedingly rare in Europe?

In his eagerness to get his findings published in a prestigious journal, Denis had chosen the wrong one, and it was too soon. He would have to wait another two-and-a-half years until an article he wrote jointly with Greg O'Conor for the American journal, *Cancer*, hit the medical world like a bombshell. In the meantime his family was due for a spot of leave.

CHAPTER 6

A New Approach

At the end of 1959 Denis Burkitt returned from leave with his family with mixed feelings. Only his mother had been at Laragh to greet them when they had arrived home in May that year. Father had died in March. Now, as they drove away from Laragh, Denis knew he would not see his mother again in this life. She had no desire to linger on alone.

So there was sadness and tears. But there was also excitement at the prospect of getting back to his surgical work, and his lymphoma research. At least his time at home had given him an opportunity to tell his first audience outside Uganda of his discoveries. Not that the doctors at Downpatrick Hospital in Northern Ireland were any more excited about them than readers of the *British Journal of Surgery*.

He returned to Mulago to a heavy surgical schedule among the Africans he had learned to love and care for deeply. As a member of the board of governors, he also had responsibilities in guiding the Mengo Hospital, which was going through difficult times. In addition he was chaplain's warden of Kampala's All Saints' Anglican Church and secretary to the Mission to Asians.

But his preoccupation was with finding out more about the distribution and cause of his lymphoma. And he was still keen to get his findings more widely known. Together with Dr Greg O'Conor, one of the pathologists of the Makerere College Medical School, Denis prepared a second expanded version of the paper published the previous year. Greg also wrote a 'companion paper' on the pathology of the disease.

This time the right journal was chosen, the American Cancer Society's widely-read *Cancer*. Publication of the paper in the 1961 March/April issue can fairly be described as a bombshell in the world of cancer research.

Greg O'Conor carefully outlined the features which made this tumour distinct from any other. Denis supported this description with his own clinical and epidemiological observations relating to age and geographical distribution, pointing out that the cancer could attack African, Asian and even European children with equal viciousness. It was this revelation, that the lymphoma was a form of cancer which had environmental rather than genetic or racial origins, that created an explosion of interest.

From the 'backwoods' of Africa, Denis Burkitt and his colleagues were providing evidence for the first time that a form of cancer might be related to climatic factors. Although it had long been recognized that various environmental factors, such as tar, sunshine, and certain chemicals could cause cancer, it was an entirely new concept that climate might somehow be implicated.

A closer look at the plotted belt suggested that even within it there were areas where the tumour had not been seen. Mostly these were above 5,000 feet. Notable was the mountainous but densely populated south-west region of Uganda. But also included were the islands of Zanzibar and Pemba, off the East African coast. Just why these islands should escape, when tumours were common on the nearby mainland, could not be explained.

In his mind, Denis was forming the idea of an on-the-spot examination of at least a part of the lymphoma belt boundary. Such a detailed first-hand study of the geographical distribution was an ambitious project. Every medical establishment in the area would have to be visited and every doctor and medical worker questioned.

As he studied the maps on his wall, Denis suspected he was embarking on an entirely new approach to cancer research — a 'geographical biopsy'. Just as a pathologist might examine a removed tissue containing both diseased and normal cells for comparison (a biopsy), so his plan was to study the boundaries between the normal and the diseased zones within and around the lymphoma belt.

That was the beginning of what at the time sounded like a schoolboy adventure but which became widely known as the 'Long Safari': a 10,000-mile, ten-week trek, through East, Central and Southern Africa.

Finance, at least, proved no problem. The interest generated by his *Cancer* article ensured that his applications for funds had a sympathetic hearing. He received offers which totalled £400, including £250 from the British Medical Research Council. To Denis, with his flair for working on a shoe-string, that was a small fortune.

Three important decisions now had to be made: what area to cover; who to take with him; and when to start.

The map on the wall showed that the northern boundary of the belt, running along some ten degrees above the equator, merged into the desert country of the Sahara, Sudan and Ethiopia. This was sparsely populated country, unsuitable for a survey. The southern limit of the belt in West Africa was bounded by sea, so that too was out. In Zaire, then still the Congo, the Simba revolutionaries were on the rampage. And to the south was Angola, where a revolution was taking place and medical services were disrupted.

This left the southern part of the east side of the belt, including the tail stretching down through Mozambique. This great stretch of land offered many advantages. English was spoken over most of the area. Population was dense and there were many hospitals. The network of roads was comparatively good. There was political stability. And it was an area of vast contrasts in climate, vegetation and terrain.

Who should he ask to go with him on his safari? At first he thought of buying a second-hand car and going with just one companion. But if for any reason that person dropped out, the project would have to be postponed. A party of three would be safer. And who better to go with him than two long-standing friends, Ted Williams and Cliff Nelson — if they would come?

Dr Ted Williams and his wife Muriel had been friends of

Denis and Olive for fifteen years. The Burkitts frequently visited their mission hospital at Arua, in the poor, extreme north-west of Uganda, close to the Congo border. Ted had built the hospital largely with his own hands, using sun-dried bricks. He had a genius for improvising medical equipment, and for repairing diesel generators and cars.

Ted happened to be visiting Kampala. Would he be prepared to join such a safari? Perhaps. But he would have to return to Arua to discuss it with Muriel. In a few days Denis got his answer. Despite having made plans to go to England on leave, Ted agreed to accompany Denis. Muriel would go to England alone.

Cliff Nelson was a Canadian doctor who had turned down opportunities for a lucrative medical practice in Alberta to do as Denis had done and follow a calling to serve less-privileged people. At the time Denis told him about the safari, he was due to leave the government medical service in Uganda to take charge of a hospital of the Africa Inland Mission in Tanzania (then Tanganyika). He could fit the safari in between changing jobs.

What made the three men compatible above all was the faith and sense of calling they shared. Who would have thought that these three, driving through the African bush in an old Ford station wagon, singing hymns at the tops of their voices, were engaged in serious medical research?

Denis readily obtained permission for absence from duty with pay from his Director of Medical Services, who was also on the board of governors of Mengo Hospital. October was chosen as the best month to set out. It was the most seasonable weather for a safari — before the rains came — and it coincided with Ted's planned leave and Cliff's move to Tanzania.

A great deal still had to be planned. Denis already had his comprehensive list of addresses of doctors and hospitals throughout East, Central and Southern Africa. To these he wrote scores of letters and, from the replies, pieced together a route for his proposed adventure. He felt the old boyhood tingle of excitement prior to a long journey.

All accommodation had to be fixed in advance. Every hospital to be visited was given a date and a suggested time of arrival and departure. He prepared a book of photographs, depicting every aspect of the tumour he was investigating. This would show doctors he visited exactly what he and his friends were looking for.

Ted Williams, the missionary-cum-mechanic, was given the job of finding and equipping a suitable vehicle for the 10,000-mile trek. From a retiring missionary, who had just escaped across the northern border into Uganda from the war-ravaged Belgian Congo, Ted bought the 1953 Ford Jubilee station wagon in which he had fled. With 45,000 miles on the clock, it cost him £250. He then had to make it safari-proof.

Sheet steel was welded beneath the petrol tank, to stop it getting holed. A lockable compartment in a hideaway place was added for storing passports, permits and money. A secret circuit-breaker was wired into the ignition system, so that the wagon could be left unattended and not get stolen. Two extra spare tyres were strapped to the roof.

Enough spares were loaded to keep the wagon healthy. The same went for medical supplies. As Denis was later overheard to say: 'We took enough medicine to look after ourselves. Medically, we must have been the safest safari ever mounted in Africa. We were three doctors, laden with medical equipment, making a bee-line from hospital to hospital!'

It was planned to start the safari on 7 October 1961. Cliff Nelson's wife and young son were to stay with Olive. Ted's wife would return from England in time to join them before the three travelling doctors returned to Kampala on 15 December.

But one further important event in the Burkitt story of medical detection has to be recorded before the safari moved off. About the time the *Cancer* article appeared, Denis and his family were once again at home on leave. It was during that time, in March 1961, that Denis met Dr (later Professor) Tony Epstein for the first time.

On a previous visit home in 1957, Denis had spoken to the surgical staff and students at the Middlesex Hospital in London about the many African diseases he had encountered. Now he was asked to speak again. This time his lecture at the famous teaching hospital was inevitably confined to his lymphoma discovery: its title, 'The commonest children's cancer in tropical Africa, a hitherto unrecognized syndrome'.

Denis had been speaking for only a few minutes when Tony Epstein, a virologist from the nearby Bland Sutton Institute, suddenly realized the significance of what was being said. The speaker was offering him the missing link in his own attempts to find evidence that viruses might be implicated in the cause of at least some human tumours. It was known that viruses could cause tumours in animals. So why not in man?

After the meeting, Tony Epstein approached Denis with a request. Could he be sent specimens of tumours from Kampala, frozen and in vacuum flasks, if he paid the cost of transporting them? Denis willingly agreed. Biopsy samples would be deep-frozen immediately after removal and flown overnight to London.

It was from one of these specimens that, three years later, a new virus, destined to become one of the most talked about in the world, was identified. With the help of research workers in America, Tony Epstein and his assistants Dr Bert Achong and Dr Yvonne Barr discovered the EB (Epstein-Barr) virus, a hitherto unknown member of the herpes group and the cause of glandular fever.

Nineteen years on from the Middlesex lecture the first textbook devoted to the EB virus was published. Its editors were Tony Epstein and Bert Achong, and the first illustration it contained was the type-written notice announcing Denis Burkitt's lecture which Epstein had, on some strange impulse, plucked from the hospital notice-board after the meeting.

During that 1961 home leave Denis was also asked to speak at an open meeting in the main hall of the Royal College of Surgeons. He had been invited by Dr Bob Harris, a member of the Imperial Cancer Research Fund team which later visited Uganda. Chairing the meeting was Sir Cecil Wakely, the ICRF president. Robed in colourful gowns the platform party was led in by a mace-bearer. Denis delivered his lymphoma lecture to an audience of just twelve.

He was disappointed, not knowing that one of his audience was a world authority on the lymphatic system, Professor Robert Pulvertaft. When he retired, Professor Pulvertaft went first to West and then to East Africa to study Burkitt's lymphoma full-time.

Fifteen years after that poorly attended meeting, when Denis was speaking to a packed audience in the hall after receiving the Royal College of Surgeons' Walker Prize, a newspaper headline read: 'Burkitt has more than twelve on this occasion.'

His 1961 leave was memorable in personal ways, too. Denis's mother had now also died. Laragh became a shell of memories — for Olive and the children almost as much as for Denis.

Five years later Denis wrote:

'Although saved from the anticipation of parting that had clouded previous leaves, there were periods of deep emotion that tore my heart-strings. Much of the time was spent sorting the accumulated paraphernalia of many decades, deciding what to destroy and what to keep.'

Among the things kept were the chains supporting a swing which his father had slung between two trees, first at Lawnakilla, then at Laragh, where Denis and Robin and their children in turn had made good use of it. It now hangs from the branches of an apple tree in the garden of the Cotswold cottage to which Denis and Olive moved when he retired.

Denis's parents were buried in the graveyard of Trory Church, where they had worshipped together for thirty-five years. It overlooks a bay of Lough Erne, where his father had enjoyed yachting, fishing and bird-watching.

The saddest time of that leave for Denis was during one morning service, when he unveiled a plaque set into the church wall in memory of his parents. He had difficulty in controlling his normally strong, clear voice, and in suppressing his tears. Pain was enhanced by the realization that this was probably the last time his family would worship there.

As he spoke, pictures of his father's old friends came to his mind. There was John Reid who helped in the garden and later worked in James Burkitt's Surveyors' Department; and Ernest Winter, the most faithful member of the small group which met at Laragh each Sunday afternoon for Bible study. He wanted to mention them but could not trust himself to speak.

Leaving Laragh for the last time was also painful. He walked up the hill behind the house and stood beside the gate in the hedge. It was here, twenty-five years earlier, that he had once pondered on his future, before taking up his first residential hospital appointment in Chester.

He closed the door of the barn where everything, from potatoes and fruit to pictures and furniture, had been stored. He bowed as a token of respect and remembrance. Then good-bye to the workshop, where his father had taught him to handle tools so well. With the shutting of the workshop door, a chapter in Denis's life was closing.

CHAPTER 7

The Long Safari

The ten-week safari began as planned on 7 October 1961. It took Denis and his two friends 10,000 miles through twelve countries, from Kampala to Johannesburg and back — equal to three times across the United States. At each border crossing they could not help feeling a bit above the average tourists, as they filled in their immigration forms. 'Purpose of visit — cancer research.'

Through rain forest, endless dry bush and beautiful game reserves, the terrain ranged from the monotonous to the tortuous. At one extreme the dust-red road stretched on for hundreds of miles, with nothing to see but rocks and trees. Only occasionally did a hill break the distant horizon. At the other extreme were perilous mountain ascents, up steep escarpments and barely negotiable hairpin bends. There were also tense night-time rides along invisible tracks, with only a compass to guide them.

The weather, too, was full of contrasts. For much of the trip drought kept river levels so low that the ferries normally used for crossing could not operate. It meant going the long way round, in search of one of Africa's few bridges.

Then came the rains, causing the team on one occasion to be marooned all night in their station wagon. Swollen rivers and washed-away bridges forced them to miss completely the two tiny countries of Rwanda and Burundi. And, when even detour roads became impassable, the three travellers had to resort to freight trains to get through.

To Ted Williams' relief, the station wagon in which they travelled gave them little trouble. The first 8,000 miles were puncture-free. It had been a shrewd move letting the garage mechanics who had overhauled the station wagon feel they were playing a vital role in an important adventure. The only time the engine would not start was when Ted forgot about his secret circuit-breaker.

Neither doctors nor mechanics could have realized at that early stage just how important the safari was going to be. Denis wrote, several years later:

'Little did we dream at that time that we were participating in a journey of discovery that would have repercussions spreading around the world like ripples on a pond.'

The safari also proved to be a prototype for many future journeys of medical detection. At first these were largely confined to tracking the geographical distribution of the one type of cancer. But subsequently information was also collected on the distribution of diseases more characteristic of modern Western society — among them obesity, coronary heart disease, appendicitis, gall-stones — all common in the developed nations but virtually unknown in the rural communities of developing countries.

As Denis and Ted said goodbye to Olive in Kampala on that Saturday morning in October and drove south to meet Cliff Nelson in Tanzania (then Tanganyika), they were doing more than setting out to make important discoveries about the geography of a particular tumour. Unknowingly they were laying the foundations for an even bigger story, one of the most exciting in medical history: the discovery that people in the West, by turning their back on nature's own dietary laws, have brought on themselves many major diseases. It was one starting-point of the fibre story, about which more will be said later.

The safari's scientific aim did not prevent it being a high adventure. For Ted Williams in particular, it was a chance to fulfill a boyhood ambition — to explore the Livingstone country which lay many miles to the south of his own mission station at Arua. It was the stirring and sacrificial life-story of

Dr Livingstone which had led Ted, while still a boy, to offer himself to God for missionary service.

The three men crossed the great missionary's tracks many times in their 10,000 miles. The first was on the eastern shores of Lake Tanganyika. They drove through the narrow streets of the mud-walled Arab town of Ujiji to the spot where, ninety years earlier, under a mango tree, the exhausted doctor and the *New York Herald* reporter Henry Stanley had their famous 'Doctor Livingstone, I presume' meeting.

Further south, the three men climbed from the shores of Lake Nyasa, discovered by Livingstone, to the mountain mission church of Livingstone. Built after Livingstone's death by Dr Robert Laws, this mission became the first tangible evidence of the vision which his life inspired in those who followed him to Africa.

Then, on their way back from South Africa, they stopped at the Victoria Falls, which Livingstone had been the first European to see, as he canoed down the Zambesi River 106 years before, almost to the day. From several miles off they watched, as he had done, the plumes of spray rise hundreds of feet into the air. And, as they came nearer, they could hear the roar of this mile-wide wonder, called by the local people Mosi-oa-tunya — 'the smoke that thunders'.

Although they would be unlikely to accept the comparison, the three men on this twentieth-century safari had much in common with the great doctor. Admittedly they were never compelled to sleep on the ground month after month, exposed to drenching showers, getting the lower extremities wetted two or three times every day, living off manioc roots and meal. But each of them could have echoed Livingstone's words with complete honesty: 'I am a missionary, heart and soul. God had an only Son and he was a missionary and a physician. A poor imitation of him I am, or wish to be. In his service I hope to live; in it I wish to die.'

Appropriate, too, were those other words which Livingstone wrote towards the end of his great trans-continental journey: 'Viewed in relation to my calling the end of this geographical feat is only the beginning of the enterprise.' Burkitt's safari was certainly to prove a geographical feat, with fifty-six hospitals, clinics and mission stations visited and more than 200 recorded cases of the malignant lymphoma discovered. Equally, it was the beginning of an enterprise.

The three men called by God to serve in Africa were on their way towards finding what the head of the British Medical Research Council, Sir Harold Himsworth, was later to compare in importance with the Rosetta Stone. Just as the inscription on the Stone, found in the Nile Delta in 1799, provided the key to modern man's understanding of ancient Egyptian hieroglyphic writing, so the clues accumulated during this journey would lead to the unlocking of some of cancer's deeper secrets.

At each hospital or clinic Denis showed the staff his grim folder of tumour photos. The pictures helped them to recall any patients they had seen, and showed them what to look out for in the future. He toured the wards, asking questions about the patients — and offering advice in return when it was asked for. He hoped by a two-way exchange to encourage future co-operation with hospital staff.

He checked each hospital operation register for records of tumours. He also made notes of any other recurring diseases that called for surgery, not fully realizing just how valuable this information was going to be in the future.

In tracking down the tumour, Denis began picking up clues right from the start. He and Ted spent their first night away from home at a government rest-house at Bukoba, on the western shores of Lake Victoria. The following morning they toured the town's hospital with the district medical officer. They asked their questions and studied the register. They found plenty of evidence that jaw tumours occurred along the shores of this lake.

Next day they continued south to the Swedish Mission Hospital at Ndolage, up in the hill-country close to the Rwanda border. Although only thirty miles from the lake they had just left, they found no evidence of the tumour. Significantly, Ndolage was 1,000 feet higher than Bukoba and many of its patients came from even higher mountain regions across the Rwanda border.

From Ndolage they descended again to Lake Victoria, before turning south to meet Cliff. They planned their meeting somewhere along the single straight road that would take them through the sparsely populated country of north-western Tanzania to the shores of Lake Tanganyika. Cliff and his wife Beth had driven north from their new home at Kola Ndota. Beth would continue north, to stay with Olive in Kampala.

The men's first night all together was spent at 'an exceptionally primitive government rest-house'. In his diary Denis wrote:

'Cliff lit a wood fire under a large oil drum to heat our water for baths, and is now doing the laundry. Ted is cooking the supper on our Primus stove. We enquired whether it was possible to buy eggs or bread in the village, and were told "No". We are therefore having baked beans, biscuits, cheese, fruit and tea for supper. Tea was made in a plastic measuring-jug.'

In the hills to the north of Lake Tanganyika, bordering on the mountainous country of Burundi, no evidence of tumours could be found. By contrast, on the edge of the lake, in the town of Kigoma, some 1,000 feet lower than Lake Victoria, there was ample evidence that the tumour was frequently encountered.

The next leg of their journey, down the east side of Lake Tanganyika, was through the most sparsely populated country of the whole safari. Denis records:

'Mile after mile, ten miles after ten miles, for nearly 250 miles the road ran through monotonous African bush. Everywhere was dry as dust, brown and burnt. Driving the first 60 miles we passed just a single vehicle and the next 170 miles not even one.'

The landscape slipped by almost unnoticed. The one vehicle they passed was a truck wrapped around an acacia tree. Conversation turned inwards as the three explorers, seated side-by-side, bumped along at a careful thirty-five miles an hour.

Mostly they talked of their findings and the possible reasons behind them. All the evidence so far supported the suspicions, which had grown as Denis plotted his lymphoma map in his Kampala office, that altitude had some part to play in the way the tumour was distributed. High up, there was no trace. Low down, there was generally plenty.

Soon they were in the low-lying country at the southern end of Lake Tanganyika. It was the sort of country where, if the altitude theory held true, they should find plenty of tumour evidence. Yet, despite careful enquiry at a number of hospitals, none was found. Puzzled by this set-back, they could only record the fact and move on to other areas and other hospitals.

They drove through the high, dry bush country of northern Zambia, where tumours were rare. Then down to the green plains around the shores of Lake Nyasa where, in the district hospital of Karonga, they were assured the tumour was a common form of cancer all along the shores of the lake.

This fertile land stretched back ten miles or so from the lake-shore to an escarpment, rising steeply to a plateau. On this plateau, at the mission station of Livingstonia, 2,000 feet above the lake and a dozen miles away, the story was different again.

After the steep climb up the zig-zag road with its 112 bends they were rewarded, not only with a magnificent view across the country that is now Malawi and beyond Lake Nyasa to the Livingstone Mountains, but also with the news that tumours were unknown in this well-populated region. Not since leaving the Bukoba region had they found so great a contrast in so short a distance.

Their confidence in the importance of altitude began to be restored. But, as scientists, the absence of tumours in the low regions of Tanzania prevented them from coming to any hasty conclusions. It was not until after the safari that Denis came to realize that rainfall was also significant in determining the areas in which the disease might be expected. Only then did it register that the low-lying plains of northern Tanzania, through which they had travelled without trace of tumour, had been the driest country imaginable.

The route from Livingstonia through the Nyasaland High-lands almost as far as Blantyre, the capital of Malawi, was high country where no trace of the tumour was found. Only as they reached lower ground around this city, named after Livingstone's Scottish birth-place, did records of it reappear.

Here an invitation to address the doctors gave Denis the chance to explain his mission and gain useful information about the disease in this area of southern Malawi.

The next stretch of the journey was to have been direct to Salisbury, crossing the mighty Zambesi at Tete. But news came that the river was too low for the ferry to operate. The alternative route was across the two-and-a-half mile rail bridge, down-river at Dona Ana.

Leaving Blantyre early on the morning of Saturday 29 October, they drove along a tortuous road through the Shiré River plain. It was hot and humid. The road soon deteriorated into a track barely distinguishable from the bush country around. If the half-expected rains had come, the three travellers would have been stranded. But the weather held as they hurried to meet the scheduled freight train.

They arrived on time but the train was several hours late. All they could do was wait, thankful for the two-gallon container of drinking-water they carried in the station wagon. It was dark before the train eventually arrived and they were able to load their vehicle onto an open-sided truck.

It took just fifteen minutes to cross the longest rail bridge in the world. But it was another two hours before they could get unloaded. It was still dark. They found it hard to rest, and they were obviously not going to find any suitable accommodation for what was left of the night. Once off the train, they chose to drive on through the darkness. With inadequate maps, and a road that was little more than a track, it was a foolhardy decision. In spite of having a compass which gave them some sense of direction, it would have been easy to get lost.

In the small hours of the morning they saw in the distance a light from the office of a telegraph operator. He gave them directions how to reach the coast road. After a further fifty miles down little more than a track, dawn began to break and the road became more distinguishable. Another 100 miles brought the tired team to the coastal town of Beira in Mozambique.

At Beira they made contact with the local hospital and found evidence of the tumour occurring right along the Mozambique coast, while at their next stop, a few miles inland and a couple of hundred feet above sea level, they found that the tumour had never been seen. Again it indicated an altitude barrier, but this time at a much lower level — a significant finding.

They made their way into Salisbury in Zimbabwe (then Rhodesia) back on schedule. Then on to Lourenço Marques where they found evidence of the tumour in a most unusual way. Over the years a pathologist at the hospital there had made plaster casts of any strange diseases he had come across. Among the collection were head-and-shoulder casts of children who had been tumour sufferers.

Denis carried these casts to the flat roof of the hospital and photographed them. In the hospital he found records of no less than forty children suffering from the tumour they were investigating, complete with addresses — by far the largest number come across in any one hospital so far.

They drove on through Swaziland. Again within a few hours of each other they passed hospitals where the tumour had or had not been recorded. Then on to the sprawling industrial complex of Johannesburg. Here, at the Institute of Medical Research, the three men poured over maps showing vegetation and insect distribution in Africa. They were searching for patterns that might correspond with those beginning to emerge from the safari.

The visit to Johannesburg gave Denis the chance of another brief meeting with Dr George Oéttle. It had been this cancer specialist's certainty that no cases of the tumours had been found in South Africa that had started Denis on his search for the lymphoma boundary. (Five years later the two men were to explore New Guinea together, the only other country in the world where the tumour had been found to be endemic.)

At the time of the team's visit to Johannesburg, the professors of surgery from all the medical schools of South Africa were meeting in the city. Again Denis had the chance to explain his mission to this knowledgeable audience. He received further confirmation of what George Oéttle had already told him: that, with the exception of the northern coast of Natal, the tumour did not occur in South Africa.

Denis, Ted and Cliff had now reached the southern end of their journey. There were still many hospitals to visit on their return. But they could set off for home knowing that they had already accumulated many important clues.

The three men reached Zambia just before the rains came. Then, for the rest of the journey, it was a fight against floods, mud and disappearing roads. In Tanzania they had to resort again to the freight train. This brought them to Tabora, from where they drove north to Cliff's mission station at Kola Ndota near Shinyanga.

After leaving the train they had hoped to reach the mission hospital the same day but a violent storm forced them to spend the night marooned in their station wagon. Across the road, in what had until a few hours before been a nearly dry river-bed, now raced a torrent of water blocking their progress.

They had no alternative but to sit out the night, sleeping in snatches, stretched out on top of the luggage. They could choose either to sweat it out in the heat of the station wagon with the windows closed, or get mercilessly bitten by mosquitoes with the windows open.

Shortly after six in the morning they managed to get through the water, expecting that the last sixty-five miles to Kola Ndota would be less eventful. They were mistaken. Just a few miles further on they met a much larger river — thirty yards wide, across their path. Denis wrote:

'Ted and I waded into the stream and found the bottom piled high with sand. We decided to try a crossing but got the wagon firmly stuck about a third the way across. With the river swirling all around and up to the wagon's floor-boards we tried to dig away the sand with a spade but to no avail.

'Fearing that we would get stuck completely in the middle of the river, we managed with help to pull the wagon back onto the bank we had just left. Fortunately a group of a dozen Africans came along and helped push, as Ted raced it across to the other side.'

The three men reached Kola Ndota, tired and dirty, a little before nine on the evening of 8 December. Here they learned that the parts of Africa through which they now planned to travel before reaching Kampala were having the worst rains that anyone could remember. Bridges and whole sections of road had been washed away. Rwanda and Burundi would have to wait until another time.

Instead they chose a more direct route home, north to the port of Mwanza on the southern edge of Lake Victoria and then by steamer to Kisuma on the north-east shore in Kenya. They travelled by freight train to Mwanza where the wagon was lifted by crane onto the steamer.

After a night aboard the steamer, they arrived refreshed at Kisuma. There was just one more government hospital and a mission station straddling the equator to visit before going home. On the morning after visiting the hospital Denis wrote in his diary:

'As soon as we have breakfasted we will be starting on our last lap and the next page (of this diary), God willing, will be from home in Mulago.'

The next entry, written at the roadside, was not the one he had planned.

'Utterly and completely stuck on a detour off the impassable road between Kisuma and Uganda. Before me is a bus across the road with one side buried deep in mud so that the body is sitting on the ground. Beyond this is another bus in a ditch and beyond that a third right across the road from ditch to ditch. This has now been pulled into one ditch by a grader. Three lorries are also stuck. There is a row of cars at each end of this confusion optimistically hoping to get across sometime. It is difficult even to stand and I have fallen flat once. I have not seen roads like this since our memorable trip to Kenya in 1952. I wouldn't be surprised if we have to spend most of the day here. We left Maseno at 8.15 this morning. It is now eleven. Of course all the local populace are lining the road for the day's entertainment.'

Over one stretch of road it took them three hours to cover fifteen miles, as they were repeatedly pushed or pulled out of the mud. It meant another unscheduled night with friends at Mbale in eastern Uganda. Next day they managed to navigate a way through flooded roads, over bridges and around overturned vehicles, to reach home in time for lunch.

A traditional Ugandan welcome awaited them — palm leaves along each side of the entrance to the Burkitt home, coloured bunting flying and a 'welcome home' arch. There to greet them were the three wives, Cliff's son and Ted's daughter, and two of the Burkitts' daughters — Judy and Rachel. Carolyn Burkitt was at school in England.

The tired but happy trio had visited fifty-six hospitals and obtained information concerning twelve more by meeting doctors who had worked in them. The cost of the 10,000-mile safari, including the purchase of the wagon for £250 and allowing for its resale at £125, was £678.

CHAPTER 8

Sifting the Results

The publicity generated by reports of the safari again stirred up the interest of the medical world. Denis was asked to speak at meetings, and articles about his trip were published in Britain and elsewhere. During the first three months of 1962 scientists, research workers and surgeons from both sides of the Atlantic were calling at the Burkitts' home, on Mulago Hill.

The media came too, among them journalists from *Time* magazine and a television crew which, to the delight of Denis's daughters, spent several hours making a three-and-a-half minute film for American audiences. His diary entry for that day reveals the man.

'Gave a lecture on my lymphoma safari. Very well attended and well received. Spent considerable time with the USA television team. I must keep myself humble.'

During this time he began analyzing the results of the safari. The East African areas of the maps on his office wall were now thickly populated with some 400 home-made pins, each representing a lymphoma victim. Not only did they confirm that the spread of the lymphoma within the belt was restricted by altitude, it was also evident that the altitude barrier fell as the distance from the equator increased.

From the equator down to a line across the middle of Lake Tanganyika the tumour did not occur anywhere above 5,000 feet above sea level. South of that line and down as far as Zimbabwe, the critical altitude dropped to 3,000 feet.

But the map revealed more. South of Lake Tanganyika the

tumour was clearly confined to river valleys, lake-shores and coastal plains. Further south still, in the tail that stretched down to Lourenço Marques, it was found only in the coastal plains. A closer study showed that the tumour was in fact only to be found in areas where the mean temperature never fell below 60°F.

It was Professor Alexander Haddow, a colleague of Denis's working as director of the East African Virus Research Institute in Entebbe, who was the first to point out that what they were looking at on the map was not so much an altitude barrier as a temperature barrier.

Denis now began wishing he had been able to visit Rwanda and Burundi. Those were the two tiny countries squeezed tightly between Zaire and Tanzania which heavy rains had made inaccessible during the long safari. Here the only low-lying regions were to the south, in the plains adjacent to the northern end of Lake Tanganyika. All the rest was mountain, rising to 14,000 feet. So, although this heavily populated region was near the equator, it was relatively cool.

Early enquiries suggested that the high regions, where the watershed of the Nile and Congo was found, were totally free from this tumour. If this could be confirmed first-hand, it would prove almost beyond doubt that, although altitude was a factor limiting the tumour's distribution, *the controlling influence was temperature*. But, to be sure, Denis needed to go there himself.

For this second trip of exploration he sought the help of another of his many long-standing friends, Michael Wood of Nairobi. The two men had been founder members of the East Africa Association of Surgeons back in 1952. Since then, Wood, who was a pilot as well as a surgeon, had gone on to set up the East Africa Medical and Research Foundation, a valuable flying doctor service.

Because medical research was one of the aims of the Foundation, Denis felt able to ask his friend's help in getting quickly to Rwanda and Burundi. It would not have been an easy journey by road, even in the dry season. Wood readily agreed to help. So, in the early morning of 24 April, within a few days of his asking, Denis and an American virologist Gilbert Dalldorf, who was visiting Africa because of his interest in the lymphoma, were flown out from Entebbe Airport.

With a map perched on his lap, Denis followed closely the route of the two-hour flight: south along the western shores of Lake Victoria, west across the volcanic peaks of northern Rwanda, and down onto the plains, to land at Burundi's capital, Bujumbura, on the tip of Lake Tanganyika. By road the journey would have taken them three days.

At Bujumbura's large and efficiently-run hospital, Belgian doctors told Denis that none of their patients came from the thickly populated high-altitude regions west of the capital, and only from the plains. A search of the operations' records and pathology reports revealed no trace of tumours in these mountainous regions. Just one suspect case was found, and he did come from the thinly populated plains.

Next day the Foundation's plane carried Denis and his companion north across the border to Rwanda's capital, Kigali. Here Denis talked with doctors who had up to twenty-five years' experience in both government and mission hospitals. No, they assured him, there was no evidence of the tumour having been found anywhere in the region.

He also heard from a Belgian doctor working in eastern Zaire, the country next door to Burundi and Rwanda and in similar terrain. He had found no evidence of the tumour in any of the cancer records which he had kept over a period of seven years. And in other hospitals in the mountainous parts of eastern Zaire, among several thousand cases of cancer, the story was repeated.

Back home, Denis wrote:

'It can be concluded that this tumour syndrome is virtually unknown in the mountainous country of Rwanda and Burundi or in the adjacent hills of Zaire. Evidence in Uganda also indicates that the thickly populated hilly country in the southwest, close to the borders and topologically identical to these two countries, is also free.

'Rwanda and Burundi, together with Kigezi in the southwest of Uganda, contain populations almost equal to that of the northern and eastern provinces of Uganda, including Mengo district, most of which lies below 4,500 feet. Yet while only two possible cases have been reported in the former territories, over 200 have been recorded in the latter.

'An even more striking contrast is likely to be observed if statistics were available from territories immediately south of Lake Victoria, where six cases have been reported in the last three months in a 70-bed mission hospital. These findings underline my conviction resulting from previous experience that the tumour limits are governed by altitude which is now seen to reflect a temperature dependence.'

Denis felt that, if temperature rather than altitude was the key to the riddle, he would need to explore a country where the temperature remained above 60°F and where there were few hills. That meant going to West Africa. This vast tropical area of the African continent, with its contrasts in vegetation and rainfall and humidity, was noted for its absence of hills. In this it was totally unlike East Africa where altitude ranged from the snow-covered peaks of the 19,000-foot Kilimanjaro down to plains at lake and sea level.

His visit to West Africa would have to be a quick one. Three weeks was all he could spare for it and this time he would have to go alone. Even so, it required careful planning, with arrangements for accommodation and visits organized ahead. The trip was not without its dangers. He would be passing through country in turmoil, the result of civil war and a breakdown in communications.

Just how chaotic things could be he found out on the first stop of his journey, in Kinshasa (then Leopoldville, capital of the Congo). It was suffering the aftermath of the Simba revolution and the granting of self-government. Denis wrote afterwards:

'I have never felt so insecure anywhere. There seemed to be no competent authority. My passport was taken from me and it took nearly one whole day of the two days at my disposal to recover it. I doubt if I would have succeeded but for the help of a senior administration official at the university who knew the right contacts. Even so we had to go from office to office, miles apart, before we eventually found my passport in a bundle of others.'

His one remaining day in the capital was spent at the city hospital attached to Louvanium University. Here he learned that the tumour had been seen frequently but that all its sufferers came from outside the city boundary. It was a significant discovery but only later did he find why the city was free from the tumour.

Long after leaving Zaire Denis still remembers the sense of relief he felt as the plane took off for the 1,000-mile journey westwards to Nigeria and its capital, Lagos. It was not just because the people of Nigeria spoke English. In contrast with the officials at Kinshasa they seemed to know what they were doing.

After a night spent in an 'exorbitantly expensive' hotel, paid for by the Nigerian Health Authority, he flew east along the coast to Port Harcourt in the Niger Delta. The town was still small, not yet affected by the discovery of oil that would one day so dramatically change the whole country's way of life. Here he met with doctors in the government hospital and showed them his photograph album. Yes, the tumour did occur in this country of steamy rain-forest.

He returned to Lagos and was immediately driven 100 miles north to Ibadan University. It had one of the best-known medical schools in tropical Africa and was later to become a major centre for the investigation and treatment of the tumour. In this part of Nigeria's western region he found the lymphoma to be the commonest tumour in children.

For the next stage of his travels, 400 miles into the dry country of the northern region, Denis chose to travel by train. That way he could sense the change of scene as he moved from the tropical forest, through savanna and into country that was desert-dry, where the only vegetation was trees and there was no rain for nine months of the year. His destination was the city of Kano. Though more than three million people lived within thirty miles of the city, there was no evidence of his tumour.

From there he flew south to Jos, the only significantly hilly part of the central region of Nigeria. He stayed at a mission hospital at the southern end of the Jos Plateau. The tumour had been seen in the surrounding tropical plains but none in the cooler climate of this elevated plateau.

Next stop was Accra, capital of Ghana. Here he met again a very old friend, Cofie George. They had first met twenty-five years before, at Trinity College, Dublin, where they had both been studying medicine. Cofie was the first black man to be seen in Enniskillen, when Denis took him to his home. Now they joked and talked of those early days, recalling the look of surprise on the children's faces as Denis had taken his friend into a village school. Cofie was now a doctor, married to the daughter of the first Speaker of Ghana's parliament, following independence in 1957.

Although the tumour was found to be common in the coastal region of Ghana, it was not known in the heavily populated area around the capital city. As Denis discovered shortly afterwards, the reason was totally different but equally significant from that which explained its absence from Kinshasa. After a brief stay in Kumasi, 150 miles north of Accra, with another medical man he had first met in Enniskillen twenty-five years earlier, he headed home.

Before leaving West Africa he bought all the atlases he could find — showing climate, vegetation and population density in the countries through which he had just travelled. As he studied these on his homeward flight the message they contained came through loud and clear. Even before reaching home he knew that this latest effort in field research had taken him an important step nearer to finding the cause of the tumour.

In Nigeria, the country he had just left, his tumour was the commonest childhood cancer in the hot southern region, where rainfall averaged more than 200 inches a year. By contrast, the tumour was almost unknown in the dry savannah of the north, where the temperature was comparable but the rainfall was barely 20 inches a year.

The story was the same in Ghana, where the tumour was common everywhere except in the extreme north, where rain-fall was low. As for its puzzling absence in the area around

Accra, in the south of Ghana, the school maps showed that the city lay in a rain-shadow which meant that the rainfall in this area was very low.

In East Africa Denis's explorations had shown a clear dependence on a temperature over 60°F. Now, in West Africa, another dimension had been added: rainfall. Never before had any form of malignant tumour been shown to be so dependent on climate. This was a very unusual tumour indeed.

Back in his office, Denis filled in the wall maps with his findings in West Africa. He showed them to Alex Haddow who confirmed that if all the areas in which temperature fell below 60°F and rainfall was less than 20 inches a year were deleted from a map of Africa, it would leave an area matching the lymphoma distribution. Alex went a stage further. He asked himself what other kind of map of Africa would show a similar likeness.

As an entomologist he instinctively knew the answer. It had to be an insect map. He told Denis about a map which hung on the wall of the Institute, back in Entebbe. It showed the distribution of yellow fever over many years. The one on Denis's wall looked very much like it.

Together the two men sought out other maps of insect-carried disease distribution: sleeping sickness (trypanosomiasis), the recently-discovered O'nyong nyong fever (it means 'pain in the bones') which Haddow and the staff of the Institute had been studying. They had distribution patterns similar to that of the tumour.

Could it really be that a human cancer was being transmitted by an insect? Admittedly it was known that viruses could cause cancer in animals and that insects could transmit viruses. But no viruses had yet been shown to play a role in human cancer. So the suggestion of a human cancer virus carried by an insect was attractive to a scientist. But it had to be treated with great caution. Its implications went far beyond Burkitt's tumour.

Only once before could Denis recall speculation that an insect might be behind the tumour. Dr Bill Davis, the head of Uganda's medical services and the man who had agreed to his paid leave for the safari, had remarked that Denis's map resembled one showing yellow fever distribution.

Over the months that followed Denis discussed with his colleagues a number of possible explanations for a link between insect and tumour. Each hypothesis was examined thoroughly in turn, and in turn discarded in the light of conflicting evidence. Other scientists around the world took up the challenge. They came from London, New York and Paris, Stockholm and Sydney, eager to be the first to find that viruses could cause cancer in humans.

To keep the flow of information concerning the lymphoma's whereabouts coming in, and to ensure a supply of specimens for investigation by virologists in Mulago, Entebbe and London, Denis and his colleagues established a search and follow-up programme. It meant keeping in touch with district hospitals over a wide area. Each hospital was sent a leaflet detailing the information Denis wanted. It was also arranged for him to be contacted whenever a lymphoma patient appeared at any one of the hospitals.

Follow-up proved more difficult than the initial search. New patients sent home after being examined and treated were told to report back for re-examination after four to six weeks. All expenses would be met. Many of them did not show up. The laboratory at Mulago would carry out its tests on a biopsy taken from the patient, only to find that the poor child had been taken back home into the bush by his or her family.

Sometimes, if the Mulago orderly specially trained for the purpose found a child and family he was able to persuade them to return to the hospital. But more often he could do no more than report to Denis on the patient's condition. Denis would then often travel into the bush to examine the patient there.

The biopsy material taken from each patient was divided into three samples: one for Mulago's own pathology laboratory, one for the virus research station at Entebbe, and one for Tony Epstein in London. It was from a sample sent to London that Dr Epstein succeeded in growing the tumour cells from which EB virus was isolated in 1964.

But it was not until 1966 that a hypothesis was found

concerning the lymphoma that would stand up to close examination. In that year a link was discovered between the distribution of the lymphoma and the immuno-depressant effect of intense malaria on a patient's defence mechanism. The ever-present EB virus would cause a proliferation of certain lymphoid cells that could then be turned into malignant cells under the immuno-depressant effect of intense malaria.

Such a hypothesis explained why the distribution of particularly intense malaria and the lymphoma in Africa and in other places like Papua-New Guinea coincided — and why the islands of Pemba and Zanzibar, off the coast of East Africa, and the areas around Kinshasa were free of the tumour. These were all places where intensive control had brought freedom from malaria and the mosquito that carried it.

All this fine detective work stimulated other scientists to begin laboratory experiments to test the hypothesis that resulted from the findings of Denis and his colleagues. Denis himself became more concerned with finding a cure for this dread disease that was disfiguring and killing the children around him. His efforts were to have spectacular results, for the oddest reasons.

In the meantime he had other more personal problems that needed to be solved. They related to his medical career and his future as a surgeon in Africa. They came to a head in June 1962, just a couple of weeks after Denis had returned from his fact-finding tour of West Africa.

CHAPTER 9

Unsettling Days

On 22 June 1962, just two weeks after returning from West Africa, Denis was at home having lunch with his boss, Dr Bill Davis, Director of Medical Services in Uganda. During the meal Bill Davis seemed more serious than usual. He began quizzing Denis. Had he thought at all about his future career?

With Uganda's independence planned for later that year, pressure was already coming from the country's Ministry of Health to turn over as many medical jobs as possible to African doctors. The days of the European expatriate were probably numbered. Bill Davis advised Denis to give serious thought to the possibility that he might have to resign his job as consultant surgeon at Mulago Hospital.

Denis had no reason to be surprised. After all, he and his colleagues in the Ugandan Medical Service had been working all these years to put themselves out of jobs. Mulago Hospital was attached to the Medical School at Makerere College where he and his colleagues had spent time training Africans as medical officers and medical assistants and turning local doctors into competent surgeons. Nevertheless he was unprepared for Bill's suggestion. After sixteen years in Uganda he was having to face, for the first time, the possibility of leaving the country.

What would he do if he had to resign and return to England? At fifty-one there was no hope of getting a surgeon's job. His medical knowledge was broad but he had no specialist experience that would be of use back home. Again he fell back on his firm conviction, proved so many times from experience, that God would overrule. That evening he wrote in his diary: 'Not really worried. The Lord will open the way.'

He could not have foreseen just how wonderfully the way was already being planned. It would be another four years before the Burkitts left Uganda. But the groundwork for a second brilliant and productive career was already being laid — even before his first one had reached any kind of conclusion.

Just two weeks after his lunch-time conversation with Bill Davis, Denis was approached by his closest colleague, Ian McAdam, head of the department of surgery at Mulago. He too was having to face the possibility of one day being redundant. He too had been thinking about Denis's future. He asked him if he had considered going full-time into a study of geographical medicine, expanding on the work he had already been doing on the distribution of the tumour?

Denis's thoughts went back to his early days in Uganda, in the up-country district of Lango. He recalled his casual observation that hydrocele was common in the east of Lango but rare in the west. He remembered the visits he had made to outlying villages; the men lined up by the chiefs to be examined; and his first-hand discovery that 30 per cent of the men in the east of the country suffered from the disease but only 1 per cent in the western areas.

He had also visited the West Nile region to survey sleeping sickness. And in more recent years he had gained experience in geographical medicine plotting the tumour, beginning with his first search of the records at Mulago and the diaries of Albert Cook, then the postal surveys and finally the safaris into tropical Africa — perhaps the most disease-ridden continent in the world.

Over the years he had made hundreds of valuable medical contacts throughout Africa and in other parts of the world. Already he had set up the information-collecting network needed to research the distribution of other diseases. But who would support such work? That was the crunch question. Denis wrote in his diary that day:

'Discussed Ian's suggestion with Olive and prayed about it. The idea is probably to provide an opening for an African.

Olive felt that 1 Samuel chapter 10 was in the form of guidance.'

This chapter in the Old Testament tells how, when God chose Saul to work for him, his instructions came through the prophet Samuel. They were step-by-step instructions, the way God's guidance is so often portrayed in the Bible.

The following day Denis wrote again: 'Feeling at peace over Ian's suggestion.'

Unknown to him, Sir Ian McAdam was already planning to write directly to Sir Harold Himsworth, head of the British Medical Research Council in London, setting out his ideas for Denis's future.

During the next few months, leading up to the independence celebrations in October, life was dominated by large and small events unconnected with his future. There were the successful and unsuccessful operations, the problems and joys of church life, the social commitments and the prison meetings and Bible studies. On top of all that, Denis was making a film about the tumour.

There was also the upheaval of moving to a new hospital. A new Mulago Hospital, the most modern in Central Africa, had been completed at a cost of £2.3 million. It now overshadowed the original, single-storey group of buildings which had stood on the site for fifty years.

The new hospital was to be opened by the Duchess of Kent, when she came with her husband to represent the Queen at the Independence celebrations in October. Plans were well under way for the handing-over ceremony. Denis had been appointed official physician to their Royal Highnesses.

During August, the presidents of the Edinburgh and the English Colleges of Surgeons visited Mulago to see the new hospital. In a small lecture theatre, with the two presidents Sir John Bruce and Sir Arthur Porritt seated in the front row, Denis and his colleagues paraded before them examples of some of the diseases they were not likely to find in their Edinburgh and London consulting-rooms.

There were hippopotamus bites and gross hernias that almost reached the knees — and four children who between them had sixteen jaw lymphomas. That was as many as Denis had been able to find in all medical literature when he had begun his search six years before. Since then his surveys had revealed over 400 in Africa alone.

By this time he was receiving invitations from all over the world to lecture about his researches. It was that same August he received his first invitation to speak in the USA, at a conference on viruses and cancer to be held the following year in Houston, Texas. And in September he flew to Johannesburg to deliver the opening address at the biennial meeting of the South African Association of Surgeons.

Then came the October independence celebrations. Denis and Olive were both there at midnight on the 8th, as the Union Jack was lowered. The job of running the country was passed to the Ugandans. During the week that followed, Denis and Olive went to a state ball, saw the opening of the new parliament, attended a garden party and a royal reception, and visited the Murchison Falls and the Queen Elizabeth Game Park with the royal party. They flew back to Mulago in time for the opening of the new hospital by the Duchess of Kent.

As he welcomed the Duchess to the hospital, Uganda's minister of health, Dr Lumu, spoke of the research work carried out at the medical school. Among the most notable, he said, was the investigation into a tumour which attacked children in Africa and was known unofficially as Burkitt's tumour — 'A fitting tribute to a man who has done so much research into it.'

The next time Denis met the Duchess of Kent was twenty years later when, as Chancellor of Leeds University, she conferred on him an honorary degree of Doctor of Science.

Shortly after the visit, Denis and Olive met two people who were to become close friends and play an important part in their lives in future days. Ralph Blocksma was a plastic surgeon. He and his wife Ruth had both been missionaries in northern India before it became Pakistan. They were visiting Mulago from their home in Grand Rapids, Michigan. It was a home that Denis and Olive would get to know well on their future visits to North America.

Towards the end of 1962 Denis spent much of his 'spare time' writing. He had been asked to contribute an article to the British magazine *The New Scientist*, dealing with the tumour and its relationship to climate. In this article, published the following January, he wrote:

'This tumour in tropical Africa has attracted attention largely because it has turned out to be an illustration in human experience of phenomena observed in animal experiments and propounded in theory by workers in other parts of the world. Although several cancers in animal and birds have for long been known to be virus-induced, no human cancer has yet been shown to be caused by a virus. This may well be the first.

'Moreover if the identification of the cause of this cancer and its means of transmission can be successfully concluded, the new knowledge is not only likely to suggest means of fighting this particular disease but may also shed light on the general problem of human cancer.'

This possibility, that the specialized work of Denis and his many colleagues might throw some light on the cause of cancer in general, increasingly attracted the attention of the popular press. Many headlines throughout the world made great play of the possible connection between cancer and an insect.

There was much talk of a breakthrough in cancer research. But more important in medical circles was the lesson of the role of good personal relationships and communications between workers. At the time the Director of the British Cancer Council, Graham Bennette, wrote with reference to research on the tumour:

'It will probably never be justified to talk about a "breakthrough" in cancer research in the way suggested by some over-enthusiastic reporters, but if ever there were an international communications breakthrough, I think it is Burkitt's tumour that must be seen as the spearhead. From East Africa to London, to Stockholm and Paris, to New York and New Guinea, to Bristol and Philadelphia, to Australia and Minneapolis, and back again to Africa the dialogues are carried on between every kind of specialist — physicians, radiotherapists, surgeons, pathologists and statisticians. This is an extraordinary phenomenon of communication . . .'

One result of *The New Scientist* article was the creation by the Australian daily newspaper, *The Age*, of a cartoon strip illustrating the story of the tumour's discovery and the possible connection with a virus carried by an insect.

The appearance of the cartoon in the paper on two consecutive days caused much amusement among Denis's colleagues. Completely out of character, Denis was portrayed as a burly bush doctor with heavy, black beard. Alex Haddow offered a possible explanation for the form of caricature: 'I think it's fairly simple. They have obviously confused you with Albert Schweitzer.'

Denis was also asked to prepare three papers for a conference organized by the International Union Against Cancer to be held in February 1963, dealing with 'Tumours of the lympho-reticular system in Africa'. The tumour he had been studying came into this category.

Denis and two of his colleagues from the Makerere Medical School had been asked to participate in the conference. Initially it was planned to hold it in Dakar, capital of Senegal, on the West African coast. Denis hit on the idea of again asking the help of the East African Medical Research Foundation to get them there.

The combined travelling expenses of the three men would cover the cost of the trip, and flying by private plane would give them the chance to stop off at a number of medical centres along the 3,000-mile route.

It was an exciting plan, but it was not to be. Because of the South African government's apartheid policy, no delegates from that country would be given visas to allow them into Senegal to attend the conference. Much to Denis's disappointment, the venue was changed to UNESCO House in Paris. He had to be content with a commercial airline as far as Rome and a long train journey to a cold Paris.

Fortunately he had bought new warm clothes before leaving home. These, and the warmth of the fellowship among old friends including George Oéttle, made up for the coldness of the city. The aim of the conference was to compare the frequency of malignant tumours of the lympho-reticular system in Africa with their frequency in Europe and the United States. Inevitably Denis's tumour dominated the papers and the discussions which followed.

Expert pathologists from around the world acknowledged that they were discussing a newly-described disease. They could not agree what sort of tumour it was, but they knew it was time to give it an official name. What should they call it?

Had it then been known that the tumour grew from a particular cell in the lymphoma's system, the 'B' cell, it would undoubtedly have been called the B cell lymphoma. But it was not, so there was general failure to agree on its true nature. In the end, it was accepted that it should be officially called by the name by which it was commonly known in Africa, Burkitt's tumour.

It was not until months later that Denis discovered his eldest daughter Judy had already written in her school-girl diary: 'They ought to call it Burkitt's tumour'! As more became known about its origins, the rather meaningless term tumour was changed to lymphoma — and, as Burkitt's lymphoma, it has been linked with his name ever since.

The day after the Paris conference ended, Denis was on his way to America. Flying first to New York, he again met Gilbert Dalldorf, the virologist from the Sloane-Kettering Institute who had accompanied him on his flying visit to Rwanda and Burundi. Then he went on by train to New Orleans and by plane to Dallas. Here he briefly visited the Parkland Hospital to examine a boy suffering from his tumour; one of the few ever to be seen in the Western world.

The same day, after an interview with the *Dallas News*, he flew to Houston. It was from here that the invitation had come the previous August to attend the seventeenth Symposium on Fundamental Cancer Research. It was sponsored by the University of Texas M.D. Anderson Hospital and Tumour Institute.

Denis Burkitt's lecture was scheduled for the third day of the conference. For the first two days he sat and listened, 'understanding virtually nothing', he confessed in his diary. By contrast, the story he had come to tell of the tumour that was killing children in Africa, and of its possible link with an insect, was understood by everyone.

By the time he got up to deliver his lecture he had already received good coverage in two Houston dailies with headlines proclaiming: 'Africa Child Cancer, Mosquito Link Seen' (*Houston Post*) and 'Scientist Hot on Trail of Cause of a Rare Cancer in Children' (*Houston Chronicle*). Both papers picked up the fact that, of the thirteen cases of lymphoma seen outside Africa, one of them was just 200 miles away in Dallas.

Before leaving Houston for New York and London, Denis visited Galveston on the Gulf of Mexico, where he lectured at the Medical School and spoke to the Christian Medical Society. While in Houston he was also made an honorary citizen of the state of Texas.

Back in London he stayed with his brother Robin before they drove down to Tetbury together to see Carolyn, who was at Westonbirt School. He returned alone to London to keep an appointment with Sir Harold Himsworth, head of the Medical Research Council. Sir Harold had offered to meet Denis and discuss a possible future for him with the Council. The interview was one more stage in a series of events which had begun the previous year with Sir Ian McAdam's letter to the MRC.

Of Sir Ian's part in these events Denis recalled in later years: 'I was to learn subsequently that Ian used the blarney I was so often accused of to put to Sir Harold that he must not miss the opportunity of appointing me.'

After another interview in London, four months later, that is exactly what happened. Denis became an employee of the MRC, resigning his job as consultant surgeon at Mulago Hospital to make way for trained African surgeons. But it was no great upheaval. He kept his teaching job at Makerere Medical School. He did not even move his office. Nor did he stop his cancer surgery or lose charge of his lymphoma patients. This was most important, because his efforts at achieving a cure for the lymphoma through the use of chemotherapy were beginning to show some amazing results.

CHAPTER 10

A Cure!

Until the beginning of 1965 reports in the medical and lay press about Burkitt's lymphoma concentrated almost exclusively on its cause. Only occasionally was any mention made of successes in finding a cure. One such rare occasion followed the 1963 Paris conference. Denis was being interviewed by the editor of *Cancer News*, a journal of the International Union Against Cancer. In answer to the question, 'What is the response to treatment?' he replied:

'Dramatic. But of course follow-up in Africa is very difficult, so that we cannot say whether the treatment we have been using has any lasting effect. At least two of our patients are symptom-free after three years. The trouble is, we have had to go out and search for these patients after treatment, so there may be very many more we don't know about who have responded well.'

Behind that brief revelation lay a most unorthodox story concerning the discovery of a medical cure. The realization, back in 1956, that the two children with swollen jaws at Mulago and Jinja hospitals were not isolated cases but representative of many other sufferers, made Denis determined to find, not just the cause, but a cure as well.

His reasons were as much humane as scientific. The sight of these and other little children, their faces distorted and swollen far beyond recognition, was deeply distressing. As a doctor he was also aware that behind the disfigurement was intense pressure caused by the rapidly growing tumours, which could double in size every forty-eight hours. Bones were destroyed, teeth pushed out, breathing was made difficult and eating impossible, until a precious young life was painfully and slowly extinguished.

Cancer can be treated in one of three ways. The methods can be used singly or in combination. The oldest of them is surgery. It can work well on isolated and easily accessible tumours. The jaw tumours were certainly accessible. But unfortunately it was soon discovered they were not isolated. The cancer which caused them was already active in other parts of the body — the liver, the kidneys, the ovaries or testes.

Early on, Denis had tried surgery. It was the only thing he could do. But at best it merely prolonged the child's life by a few months. Gross facial disfigurement was replaced by unsightly scars. It was never long before the tumour recurred, or manifested itself in other parts of the body.

The second method for removing cancer, a method widely used in the Western world with great success, is radiotherapy, in which X-rays are concentrated to destroy an accurately located cancerous growth. The rapidly multiplying cells of such a growth can be killed because they are far more vulnerable to the X-rays than normal body cells.

The problem with X-rays is that unless the dose of radiation is carefully controlled it will kill normal cells as well. Control is fairly easy when the cancer is on the surface of the body. Deep-seated cancers require a more careful balance to be maintained. One solution is to bombard the deep-seated cancers from several directions, the separate beams all converging at one point.

For Denis, the problems that came from using X-rays were academic. He had no radiotherapy. In fact, from Cairo in the north of Africa to Salisbury near the south, a distance of 3,000 miles, there was no radiotherapy available in any part of tropical Africa at that time. Not until 1968 was a radiotherapy unit installed in East Africa.

The third method of treating cancers is chemotherapy, the use of drugs that destroy the cancerous cells, with or without the aid of the patient's own defence mechanisms. Used on its own it was not usually very successful. Burkitt's lymphoma was to be an exception. In fact, until the 1960s, only one other form of cancer could be cured by using chemotherapy alone, a rare cancer of the womb which starts growing in the placenta.

The advantage of chemotherapy is that the drugs reach every part of the body through the bloodstream. So it was appropriate treatment for Burkitt's tumour, which was known to be widely spread throughout the body. But, as with X-rays, it was difficult to control the dosage to ensure that it killed the cancer cells without doing serious harm to normal cells. Also, the side-effects on blood cells and other cells that multiply quickly, such as those in the hair follicles and the lining of the intestine, could be severe. Any prospects of cure had normally to be balanced against the cost of treatment in terms of suffering.

For Denis, no such balancing act was necessary. Surgery alone could never be successful. And there was no access to radiotherapy equipment. So the answer had to be chemo-therapy. But there were two serious problems to be overcome. In the first place, his experience in applying chemotherapy was nil. And in the second place, he had no money with which to buy the additional drugs, which were expensive.

As with many of the professional problems which Denis had faced in the past he solved these two by a combination of single-minded determination and the willingness of other people to give help. But such willingness is not always to be taken for granted amongst people in medical research. All too often people cling jealously to their skills and hard-won knowledge, using them for their own advancement.

For the purchase of drugs he could not expect much help from Mulago Hospital. Uganda's economy was such that hospitals could barely afford drugs for the eradication of far more widespread and economically destructive diseases. The experimental use of costly drugs would be hard to justify. So, with a characteristic piece of lateral thinking, he turned a lamentable shortcoming into a positive asset. He used the lack of radiotherapy equipment and the fact that none of his patients had been exposed to X-ray as arguments to persuade the Nairobi representative of an American drug company to supply the drugs he needed.

Just how he went about this is best told in his own words:

'I hit on the idea of writing to the manufacturers of these drugs, pointing out that almost all the patients who had been treated in the past using drugs had already been exposed to radiotherapy. In view of this I ventured to suggest that the drug companies were in no position to assess what effect their drugs were having. Any improvement might be due to a late effect of X-rays and not to the chemotherapy.

'I explained that we were in a position uniquely advantageous to them because we had no X-ray therapy. Nor was it available anywhere in tropical Africa. If they gave us some of their drugs free of charge we would gladly use them and report on their efficacy. This they willingly agreed to do and looked on me rather as a benefactor than as a beggar.'

In this way Denis was supplied with the drugs he needed — methotrexate to begin with. Next he had to learn to use them. By great good fortune, about that time — the end of 1960 — Dr Joseph Burchenal, one of the world's leading authorities on chemotherapy, visited Mulago Hospital. He was with a team of scientists from the Sloane-Kettering Institute in New York, working in Nairobi on cancer treatment using drugs at the Kenyatta National Hospital.

No doubt caught up by Denis's enthusiasm, Joe Burchenal willingly gave him guidance in the use of the drug. Basically, he told him, the patient had to be given the maximum dose possible, short of killing him. This would offer the best possible chance of destroying the tumour while keeping the patient alive.

The side-effects of such treatment were severe — the depletion of blood cells, internal bleeding and loss of hair. It meant the patient's blood had to be examined every day and the treatment stopped as soon as danger level was reached.

Denis began his experimental treatment on two young boys, Israeli and Kibakola. They were both given tablets to swallow at intervals throughout the day. Israeli had a huge tumour of his left upper jaw. After a quite small dose of treatment this shrank, almost miraculously. But it kept recurring, despite repeated doses.

The boy would wander over on his own to the Burkitts'

house, close by the hospital — a constant reminder of Denis's apparent failure. Eventually he died. At only one other time do Denis's daughters recall seeing their father so visibly distressed and that was when he learned of his own mother's death.

In contrast, Kibakola's tumour completely disappeared and never recurred. Denis kept in touch with him for six years, until the Burkitts left Uganda. Encouraged by this success, he began treating other children. Very soon, as he later put it, the 'most inexperienced chemotherapist in the world was getting the best results'. This was particularly odd, since he was often unable to administer the drugs at the level which the experts said was necessary for successful treatment. For one thing, since it was difficult to monitor patients adequately, it was thought unwise to work close to the toxic limits of the drugs. Sometimes the pressures of his other duties gave him too little time to attend his children. But more often those being treated would be spirited away by their parents, even in the middle of the night, with the treatment hardly begun.

One seven-year-old girl left after receiving one sixth of the scheduled methotrexate dosage. When a hospital assistant found her at her home in the bush a year later she was in perfect health. Not only was Denis curing the children of their tumours, he was doing it with drug doses so low that they caused none of the expected nasty side-effects.

He had similar successes with other drugs given to him for nothing. With cyclophosphamide he was getting 50 per cent cure rates, mostly on patients with no clinically detectable tumours other than in the jaws. Why such spectacular results on inadequate doses?

Two reasons were subsequently found for the surprising success. Partly it was because Burkitt's lymphoma was the fastest-growing tumour in humans. Every cell divides every day. And it is when the cell divides that it is most vulnerable to the highly toxic chemicals in the drugs applied. So, with Denis's treatment, each dose of the drug was hitting all the cells during division, thus rapidly destroying a high proportion of them.

But an even more important factor was the unusual strength

of the patient's own defence mechanism, which can fight off attacks by foreign bodies including certain cancer-cells. When the body is subjected to the massive doses of a drug that most chemotherapy requires, the drug may knock out many cancer cells but at the same time it may depress the patient's own defence against the tumour.

In contrast, by supplying drugs in small doses, Denis was destroying just enough of the tumour to enable the patient's own defence mechanism to deal with the rest. Soon he was getting complete and often sustained remission with just one or two injections. The fact that the body's defences responded so well to the drugs was another indication that the cause of the tumours was a foreign body — a virus.

With the exception of the rare womb cancer, choriocarcinoma, already referred to, Burkitt's tumour remained until the mid-1960s the only tumour which could be cured in a high percentage of patients by chemotherapy alone.

One of the last tasks which Denis undertook before he left Uganda in 1966 was to organize, in co-operation with Dr Joe Burchenal, an international conference on Burkitt's tumour, with the emphasis on treatment. The conference, chaired jointly by Denis and Joe Burchenal, was the idea of the Chemotherapy Panel of the International Union Against Cancer, the union which at its previous conference, three years earlier, had decided officially to adopt the name Burkitt's tumour.

At one session of the 1966 conference Denis stood up to challenge in a dramatic way the accepted idea that chemotherapy in the treatment of tumours always demanded the maximum reasonably safe dose. Weeks before he had gone to great trouble, arranging for twenty-three children who had been cured of the tumour by drugs to be brought from their homes. Some travelled long distances to stay at Kampala during the conference.

During the session he paraded the children one by one in front of his audience of surgeons, doctors, virologists, pathologists and chemotherapists. The audience was given notes containing brief details of each child, including a photograph showing his or her condition before drug treatment began. It was a presentation that greatly moved men whose professional lives had been spent close to suffering.

When the proceedings of the conference were published the following year they contained an addendum submitted by Denis. It included a photograph taken at the conference and showing one group of healthy-looking long-term survivors. There were also pathetic pictures of what four of these children looked like before treatment. Little wonder this group of authorities was moved by what it had seen.

The feelings of the delegates were summed up in a closing address made by Sir Alexander Haddow FRS*, the president of the UICC which had arranged the conference:

'I have been in the field of cancer research for nearly forty years. During this time I have attended hundreds of scientific meetings. With the utmost sincerity I can say that never have I attended a conference more fruitful or more inspiring than this. No one who witnessed it can ever forget yesterday's demonstration of Burkitt's patients — cured African children, we hope. It was an experience expressly moving and of the utmost practical significance, not only for these children and their parents and families, but also for us in proving that gross pathology can be reversed by purely chemical means.'

He closed his speech, and a memorable conference, with the words:

'I add a further word of tribute to Burkitt, a tribute we must all share — to him as an outstanding surgeon and, I would say, physician. An outstanding observer and researcher. But perhaps, beyond all else, what has most impressed us rests in his kindliness and in his humanity towards his patients. We are all very proud of him.'

It was a speech that could be regarded as a fitting climax to Denis Burkitt's professional career, working amongst Africans for twenty years. As the conference ended there was general agreement that the long-term remissions which he had been achieving were probably the result of the combination of chemotherapy and the patient's own defences.

*Not the Dr Alex Haddow who had first spotted the similarity of Denis Burkitt's lymphoma map with that of the tsetse fly and yellow fever.

Denis himself said: 'The dramatic successes which we seem to have achieved are probably due to the fact that we have disobeyed some of the conventional rules of chemotherapy by not giving the maximum dosage.'

Two years after the conference, a special centre was set up at Mulago Hospital for the treatment of Burkitt's lymphoma. Dedicated to Denis Burkitt, it was run by Dr John Zeigler, who took over where he had left off. In contrast to Denis, Dr Zeigler, who came from the National Cancer Institute in Bethesda, outside Washington, was an acknowledged authority on chemotherapy. He was able to use a variety of drugs in different combinations to assess the best treatment in different circumstances. He had outstanding success in treating the tumour. He was also able to study the immunological aspects of the tumour, so discovering how the patient was able to use his own defence system to overcome the tumour cells in his body.

Zeigler, too, eventually left Uganda. He became director of chemotherapy at one of the world's leading centres for the investigation and treatment of cancer, the National Cancer Institute in Bethesda, Maryland, USA. It was at this Institute twenty-six years after discovering the existence of the tumour, that Denis addressed a famous audience. In a speech given after he had received the 1982 General Motors Cancer Research Foundation Mott Prize for his tumour research, he listed the following four lessons learned.

The first was the importance of clinical observation: 'Much valuable information can be learned during the course of routine clinical duties,' he said, 'not only in large hospitals but in small district hospitals in the third world and in the surgeries of country practitioners.'

The second was the defects of specialization: 'One of the major defects of cancer research is specialization in cancer. Valuable clues to cancer causation can be found through examining the distribution of non-malignant diseases that appear related to a particular form of cancer.' (In the case of Burkitt's lymphoma it was the realization that there was a link between the distribution of the lymphoma and of malaria.)

The third was the role of simple observation followed by

deductive reasoning: 'Sophisticated technology and especially computers can overshadow the simple use of observations and deduction in approaching the problems of disease causation.'

The fourth was the fallacy that fact-finding is directly related to funding: 'The cost of the initial investigation that revealed the lymphoma belt was £25. For the long safari the accounts prepared afterwards showed that with the purchase and sale of the station wagon the cost came to £678 for a ten-week 10,000-mile journey.'

On this occasion he did not go on to mention the fact that the drugs with which he had discovered how to cure the tumours cost him virtually nothing. What he did say was how much he owed to the loyalty and generosity of his colleagues, from missionary doctors working in isolation to professors working in major teaching hospitals.

Towards the end of his address he asked: 'Was I in fact any more than a catalyst in the process?' Most people who worked with him would say without hesitation that he was a good deal more. Even so, the Denis Burkitt story is the story of a great many other people as well. On numerous occasions he has publicly acknowledged his debt to so many whose names do not appear in these pages.

In the same way, there are many other scientists and medical workers who owe their medical discoveries and their reputations to Denis Burkitt's pioneer work on the lymphoma. There was that one discovery in particular where all concerned acknowledge him as the catalyst. The discovery of the Epstein-Barr virus and its consequences already has a whole library of literature to its credit and, as a spin-off from the Burkitt story, it deserves a chapter of its own.

CHAPTER 11

The EB Virus

The discovery that Burkitt's lymphoma depended on climate and that it might be caused by a virus, gave renewed impetus to the search for a viral cause of other forms of cancer. Ever since 1908 it had been known that viruses were responsible for some animal cancers. In that year two Danes, Ellerman and Bang, showed that leukemia in chickens could be transmitted by a virus.

Three years later, at the Rockefeller Institute for Medical Research in America, Peyton Rous found that a solid form of cancer in chickens could also be caused by a virus. Subsequently it was discovered that viruses caused cancer in many different animals, even in some monkeys. It led to an ongoing quest for evidence that at the back of some human cancer there might be a virus.

Now the question was being raised again. Was there a human cancer virus? Could there even be a virus which under the right conditions, or together with another virus, might initiate cancer in people? This possibility had the world's cancer researchers knocking on Denis Burkitt's door at Mulago Hospital. They were requesting tumour samples from which they hoped to be the first to find the hidden cancer germ.

Two groups of British researchers had a head-start on the rest. They were Tony Epstein's team, working at the Bland-Sutton Institute in Central London, and Bob Harris and his workers from the Imperial Cancer Research Fund at Mill Hill. As early as 1961 both men had seen that the peculiar geographical distribution of the tumour suggested the possibility of a virus origin: Harris after reading the article in *Cancer*, and Epstein as a result of hearing Denis speak that day at the Middlesex Hospital.

By the end of 1961 Harris, with two of his technical assistants from the ICRF's virology division, had set up his laboratory at the East African Virus Research Institute in Entebbe. It should have been sooner but there had been some official heel-dragging at head office. How they eventually managed to get to Entebbe provides an insight into the competitive pressures which are to be found even in cancer research. Harris believed he needed to carry out research in the field but he had great difficulty in getting the money to ship his laboratory equipment out to Uganda. Not until it was learned in London that workers from America had already arrived in East Africa was the urgency of Harris's request appreciated. Then, to make up for lost time, wheels-within-wheels began to turn and the air force was persuaded to fly the equipment out.

Like Denis, and so many others in this story, Bob Harris was a devout Christian. Until his death he and Denis remained firm friends. Denis later wrote about him: 'He was a leading authority in the field of cancer causation. His obituary in *The Times* cited his academic honours and appointments held. But no mention was made of his deep, personal faith in God which was of much greater consequence to him, and to his family at such a time, than academic achievement and recognition.'

The outcome of Harris's work in Entebbe was the discovery that a universal virus known as Reo 3, first found by an Australian scientist, appeared to be more common in Burkitt's lymphoma sufferers than in other people. At the time there was great excitement that it might have a role in causing Burkitt's lymphoma. Subsequently it was found to be no more than a passenger. Nevertheless, a valuable discovery had been made. Certainly Denis believed it:

'Like a maze, those avenues of exploration that prove to be blind alleys can then be sealed off to avoid the need for re-exploration. So the number of possibilities remaining is reduced, to simplify the task of the man who eventually finds the right route.'

A greater flurry of excitement of more permanent importance was caused two years later, in 1964, when Tony Epstein discovered, through the electron microscope, what became known as the Epstein-Barr virus. He used tumour samples flown to London from Mulago Hospital to grow additional tumour cells by tissue culture, in dishes containing the right nutrient and held at the right temperature.

No one had ever successfully cultured human lymphoma cells before. The technique used by Epstein and his assistants Dr Yvonne Barr and Dr Bert Achong proved to be the key which unlocked this previously unknown virus. It took them two years, using twenty-four different samples, to get the cultured cells to grow. In 1963 it happened. Cultured cell type EB_1 was born, followed by EB_2, EB_3, and so on.

Under the powerful magnification of the Institute's electron microscope Epstein found these cultured cells to be carrying a virus he did not recognize. He was so excited the first time he saw it, and so afraid that the heat of the microscope could cause it to disappear, that he switched it off and went for a walk. It was still there when he came back, so he called in his staff to share in his find.

It was agreed that, although the virus looked similar to viruses belonging to a group called herpes and known to be responsible for chicken-pox, shingles and cold sores, somehow it was different. To find out why, and to establish whether or not it was in any way connected with the herpes group, Epstein turned to other virologists for help. And having failed to obtain any help in Britain he looked to people he knew abroad.

News of his ability to produce cultured lymphoma cells had already created a demand for his 'products' and among his customers were two doctors, Werner and Gertrude Henle. These two virologists worked in the virus laboratories of the Children's Hospital in Philadelphia, where as a husband-and-wife team they specialized in the study of children's viruses.

The Henles had become familiar with Burkitt's lymphoma the previous year when a medical colleague, returning from East Africa, had suggested that they might find it worth studying as a human cancer that could be virus-induced.

Within days of Epstein's discovery, the latest batch of his cells were being flown across the Atlantic to the Henle laboratory. The virus was isolated very quickly. Attempts were then made to transmit the virus to other culture cells susceptible to known viruses in the herpes group. Failure to do so confirmed that this was indeed a different and newly-discovered virus.

Next came the job of finding out if the EB virus was an active participant in the Burkitt lymphoma cells, responsible in some way for their formation, or just a passenger. If the virus was active in the formation of the lymphoma cells it would be indicated by the presence of antibodies in the blood, attempting to fight the invading virus.

These EB virus antibodies were found in all blood samples taken from Burkitt lymphoma sufferers. So the virus was definitely active. Then the Henles went on to examine blood samples from African children who had not suffered from lymphoma. Writing in the magazine *Scientific American*, in July 1979, they described what they had found:

'To our surprise antibodies to the Epstein-Barr virus were found not only in children with Burkitt's lymphoma but also in the blood samples of nearly all the healthy children tested. Even more unexpected was the finding that antibodies to the virus were present in children from many other parts of the world, which implied the EB virus has a world-wide distribution with almost no one escaping infection.'

It proved in fact to be a universal virus — what the medical world calls ubiquitous. Blood samples from Burkitt's lymphoma sufferers did, however, differ from healthy samples in containing much higher levels of antibodies, indicating that lymphoma sufferers had reacted to the virus in an abnormal way. This suggested that a continued search for a connection between the virus and the lymphoma would prove worthwhile.

The fact that the EB virus was ubiquitous suggested to the Henles that they had found the cause of some common illness. It could not be Burkitt's lymphoma, since this affected only a relatively small number of people and was largely confined to the tropics of Africa and Papua-New Guinea. So now the

Henles were on the hunt for a universal disease that would fit a universal virus. Then, towards the end of 1967, came one of those remarkable accidental discoveries with which medical research seems so fortunately strewn.

Working in the Henles' laboratory was a nineteen-year-old technician, Elain Hurtkins. In the routine course of their work they had discovered that her blood contained no EB virus antibodies. They knew this to be very unusual, since 85 per cent of all the people whose blood they had tested, American and European, as well as African, had these antibodies.

It meant that Elain had never been infected with the EB virus. Then one day she reported sick. She was away from work for a week, with all the symptoms of glandular fever — sore throat, fever and enlarged lymph glands. When she returned to work, her blood was tested again. Now, for the first time, it was found to be full of EB antibodies.

Far from being disappointed at losing a unique source of blood for their experiments, the Henles were delighted. It was the first clue that the EB virus might be the long-sought-for cause of a universal disease, glandular fever, which had first been described in 1920. It was an exciting possibility but more evidence was needed. That meant taking more blood samples from people known to have suffered from glandular fever.

The Henles remembered that the Yale University School of Medicine had been engaged since 1958 in a study of glandular fever (medically known as 'infectious mononucleosis') among college students. Hundreds of blood samples had been collected and frozen. These were made available to the Henles for examination. They found that the EB virus antibodies were always present after the disease had been contracted but never present before.

They were led to the unequivocal conclusion that the Epstein-Barr virus was responsible for glandular fever. It was an exciting and potentially very important conclusion, since finding the cause is a good first step towards finding a cure.

With Epstein's discovery of the EB virus back in 1964, Denis Burkitt had begun putting together a hypothesis based on the possibility that it was the cause of the lymphoma. All the circumstantial evidence fitted in with the ideas that the virus might be carried by mosquitoes and injected into the victims through their bites.

This latest discovery, that the virus was the cause of glandular fever, a disease found throughout the world and therefore not transmitted by an insect, meant that Denis's hypothesis was no longer tenable. It did not, however, come in time to save him from some embarrassment as a result of expressing his hypothesis in public:

'I was due to present this hypothesis at an international cancer congress at Ann Arbor University in Michigan in 1967 and was at that time reading a Sherlock Holmes detective novel. I marked the page where Dr Watson remarked to his chief that in a certain criminal case the circumstantial evidence seemed so strong that the prisoner could be considered almost certainly guilty.

'The famous detective had replied that circumstantial evidence could be very unreliable. When you looked at it from one angle it seemed to point in one direction, but if viewed from another aspect it pointed an entirely different way.

'I wondered whether these words might one day apply to my hypothesis and, as events turned out, I had to admit the errors of my conclusions even before the paper I had delivered was published. I have on many occasions publicly stated my conviction that no progress is made in medical research — or in happy marriage — unless mistakes are openly admitted.'

Denis was quite prepared to admit that his original hypothesis (that the lymphoma was caused by an insect-borne virus) was wrong, as this report in *Medical World News* for November 1968 confirms:

'Denis Burkitt, the man who first defined the jaw tumour found in Central African children and whose epidemiological mapping of the disease led him to the hypothesis that it was caused by a mosquito-borne virus, has now decided that the hypothesis was wrong.

'Last month at a symposium organized by the British Association of Cancer Research, he put forward a new theory in which malaria as well as viral infection plays an essential role in Burkitt's lymphoma. His new hypothesis runs as follows:

'"A virus, almost certainly the EB virus that has been found in nearly every case of BL, is common the world over. In normal lymphoid tissue this virus is usually harmless, but occasionally it causes a non-malignant proliferation that leads to infectious mononucleosis. On rare occasions it causes a malignant transformation and gives rise to Burkitt's lymphoma."'

So, even if the EB virus was not transmitted by an insect to cause Burkitt's lymphoma, that did not rule out the possibility that it had some role to play in combination with other factors peculiar to the environment where the disease was found. It might be an unusual or rare event following an infection of, say malaria, which paved the way for the EB virus to act in a cancer-forming way.

To test these possibilities, some forty or so scientists, including the Henles and Denis Burkitt, and a Dr Guy de-The of the International Agency for Research in Cancer, met in Nairobi at the end of 1968 to discuss setting up an experimental project similar to the one at Yale ten years earlier. The plan was for blood samples to be taken from all the young children in a region of Africa where the tumour was known to be common.

The blood would be kept labelled and refrigerated until one of the children developed a tumour. It would then be possible to discover whether or not there were EB virus antibodies in that child's blood before the tumour developed. The region chosen was the West Nile region of Uganda. This was largely because of the work of Denis's safari companion Ted Williams and his brother Peter. Both knew the area well, spoke the local language fluently and were sufficiently well-respected and trusted to get the local people's co-operation.

Dr Guy de-Thé was chosen to direct the project with an Indian, Dr Berry, responsible for its day-to-day running. Each day several teams of medical workers went out into the bush to draw blood from children gathered under the village trees. Blood samples were taken in this way from over 45,000 children, about 95 per cent of the child population between one and four years of age. The samples were refrigerated and flown to the headquarters of the International Agency for Research in Cancer in Lyon for storage.

Over the next five years fourteen of these children developed Burkitt's lymphoma. Every one was found to have had a very high level of the EB virus antibodies when originally bled. From this it was concluded that severe infection with EB virus somehow made children much more prone to developing Burkitt's lymphoma. No more precise conclusions were revealed and the search for more positive evidence continued.

In the meantime Denis could take great comfort from the fact that it was from cell cultures from his tumours that the discovery of the cause of glandular fever had come. It would ensure that his name was permanently linked with Epstein's work. Official recognition of that link came in April 1982 when Denis Burkitt and Tony Epstein were jointly selected to be the first non-American recipients for the Bristol-Myers Cancer Award. This and the General Motors Awards are the world's top awards for cancer research.

Denis saw the role he had played in the discovery of the EB virus as being like a launch-pad from which others can fire their rockets.

'My work would have remained for the most part unknown and relatively valueless had not other more knowledgeable, better equipped, and more competent people than I constructed rockets which have been successfully launched into new realms of research endeavour.

'The construction of a rocket requires infinitely more knowledge and technical ability than does the building of a launch-pad. Professor Epstein and his colleagues both in Britain and elsewhere together launched the EB virus programme, with all the ramifications that these studies have had in various fields of scientific research.'

Ramifications was right. It is doubtful if any other virus has received so much attention, or been the subject of so many articles in medical literature, since that day when Tony Epstein peered into his electron microscope and saw the EB virus for the first time. The Henles concluded their *Scientific American* article with the words: 'For those willing to accept the indirect evidence, the Epstein-Barr virus is the foremost candidate for being the first known human cancer virus.' It had all been a supreme example of scientific co-operation which began with the work on Burkitt's lymphoma.

CHAPTER 12

Last Days in Uganda

To pick up once again the more personal aspects of the Burkitt story we have to go back to the middle of 1963. Denis had attended the Paris conference at which Burkitt's tumour became officially recognized by that name. Then, following a visit to America, he had had his interview in London with the Medical Research Council.

By June he was back in Kampala, still uncertain what path his future career would take. But he was becoming increasingly convinced that in some way it would involve geographical pathology, probably plotting the distribution of cancer.

By July he and Olive were due to go home on leave to Britain. They were both in need of it. Denis's work-load was heavy, and there were continuing crises at the Mulago Hospital, as a result of the shortage of nurses. At one point the hospital was threatened with closure because so many wards were unstaffed.

Olive, as much as Denis, had always led an active life in the community in Kampala. She was a youth-work leader through the Crusaders and Girl Guides, vice-president of the Uganda Council for Women, a life member of the YWCA and a long-serving member of the young wives' group at All Saints' Anglican Church in Kampala, where Denis was chaplain's warden and a lay reader.

Both were tired at the end of their term of service, but their chief anxieties concerned their three daughters. Local schooling was available only up to the age of twelve. Judy was now sixteen. She had been away at a girls' secondary school in Kenya for four years. After independence the future of such

schools became uncertain. Denis and Olive had already sent
Carolyn to a boarding-school in England. Rachel was still in
Uganda but would not be able to stay much longer. So anxieties
about the future of the country were aggravated by the inevitable splitting up of the family. It was clear that before long
they would need to settle in England.

Following Uganda's independence there was always the
possibility that the country might break off relations with
Britain. Uganda was finding its progress towards mature
independence difficult. Differences of view between the
Kabaka, as president, and the central government, in particular
Prime Minister Obote, were creating great unrest, which three
years after this resulted in the Kabaka being driven out of the
country and Dr Obote becoming president.

As close friends of the Nabagereka, the Kabaka's wife who at
the time of independence had been dismissed from his household because he preferred her sister, the Burkitts knew only too
well how unstable the country now was. Already they could see
some of the tragic signs of the struggles for power and the
smouldering discontent that led to the 1971 coup by Idi Amin
and the atrocities that followed.

So July 1963 came none too soon for Olive and Denis. It was
agreed that when Denis returned to Mulago the following
December he would go back alone. For the sake of her health
and to be nearer the children, who by then would all be in
school in England, Olive would stay behind temporarily, in a
house they rented in Nettlebed near Henley-on-Thames.

Denis and Olive began their much-needed leave that summer
with a few days at the home of Olive's parents, with Denis
attending several interviews in London. Then came a week's
holiday at Lee Abbey in North Devon, after which they picked
up the three girls and travelled across to the west coast of
Ireland for six weeks.

There followed a few more days in London, during which
time Denis had confirmation that he had been accepted by the
Medical Research Council to work as a member of its external
scientific staff, initially in Kampala but eventually back in
England.

Then, in October, Denis and Olive left for two months in North America. For Denis it was his first coast-to-coast lecture tour: from New York to San Francisco, St Louis to Winnipeg and Edmonton. This time he was there to impart knowledge, rather than to gather it. They had been invited to America by the Director of the Sloane-Kettering Institute of Cancer Research in New York, Dr Frank Horsfall.

Despite her recent holiday, Olive was far from well. The depression that had plagued her following the birth of their third daughter, Rachel, more than ten years before, was recurring. It had been a difficult birth, accompanied in its later stages by hepatitis and jaundice. At the time there had been an epidemic of poliomyelitis attacking expatriate young people in Uganda.

Judy and Carolyn had both become unwell at the time and, although they had recovered, the experience left Olive severely depressed. Now, with the stress of preparing for the girls' schooling back in England and the tension as they arrived in America at the beginning of a hectic tour, she again fell low. To fulfil his commitments for the tour, Denis had to make alternative arrangements for Olive to be looked after.

He got in touch with the people he knew best in America, the Blocksmas in Grand Rapids. They willingly agreed to take care of her, 'looking after her like a daughter', as Denis put it.

He travelled almost continuously for six weeks, lecturing to medical schools, universities and hospitals, as well as to different chapters of the Christian Medical Society. He had his first opportunity to show to large audiences the film he had made in East Africa, depicting the clinical and epidemiological aspects of the tumour, together with some of the dramatic responses to treatment being achieved.

He enjoyed himself as he travelled around, being billed as a celebrity in some places, mistaken for a missionary in others. Everywhere he took great pains to see that others who had helped in his work were given their share of the credit. The report which appeared in the *Winnipeg Free Press* for 13 November 1963, following his visit to the Manitoba Medical

Association was typical of a number that were published during the tour:

'Dr Burkitt disclaimed credit for discovering the (virus and environment) theories, but gave praise to other men who have been active in the field including Dr J. N. P. Davies, Dr G. O'Conor, Dr Gilbert Dalldorf and Prof. Alexander Haddow, who is director of the Virus Research Institute in Uganda. The research and safaris are continuing. Britain has a medical team out in Uganda under the direction of Dr R. J. C. Harris of England, and the French have a team in Senegal in West Africa.'

When Denis visited Edmonton to give a lecture to the medical students at the University of Alberta, the local press took delight in the fact that Cliff Nelson, who had been one of the long safari team, came from Edmonton.

Back in England at the end of November, Denis and Olive had just a few more weeks to spend together before Denis returned alone to Uganda. They both dreaded yet another long period of separation, so 5 December was a black day. The previous afternoon they had walked together in the country lanes around Nettlebed, steeling themselves for the morrow.

What made the parting hardest of all for Denis was his concern for Olive.

'She had not been well, and I knew instinctively her inward fears of being left alone with all the responsibility of the family. I had never felt so torn between my love and responsibility for my family on the one hand and my research work and duties in Africa on the other. During the previous few years my work had blossomed more than ever before. There seemed to be nothing for it but to feign more optimism than I felt and to trust and pray. But saying "Goodbye" was painful in the extreme.'

Back in Mulago for Christmas, Denis was not alone. He had many friends. But he was lonely as he waited for Olive's letters, and when they came they seemed long and sad. He made numerous frustrated attempts to phone her. On New Year's Eve he received three letters and wrote in his diary: 'Another year passed. Father let me dedicate all this year to thee.'

The couple had expected to be separated, at least until after the girls' Easter holidays. They attempted to console themselves with the fact that this was only one-sixth of the time they had spent apart during the war. As it turned out it was to be even less than that.

One day early in February, Denis returned home to lunch to find his house boy Yusufu anxiously waiting for him. A doctor from England had phoned and would ring back. Denis recognized the doctor's name, and knew it was to do with Olive. He feared the worst, instinctively knowing that Olive was ill again. Later in the day the call came through. Olive was unwell and he was recommended to return home to her.

'I have never felt so low or fearful in my life. I did my best to lean on God's promises. "Cast thy burden upon the Lord and he shall sustain thee" and "Trust in the Lord with all thine heart; and lean not unto thine own understanding. In all thy ways acknowledge him, and he shall direct thy paths." Easier to say than to actually do.'

Denis immediately contacted his medical headquarters and was granted unpaid leave. Within two days he was on a plane to London. The doctor's wife met him and drove him to their home, where Olive was staying. With Denis back home she began quickly to recover from her depression. So, after a month, there was yet another parting. This time it was agreed that Olive should follow him out to Uganda at the beginning of May, after the girls' Easter holidays, by which time Denis would have settled into his new appointment and a new house.

Denis started his new appointment with the Medical Research Council officially on 1 April 1964. He kept his old office but after sixteen years at 18 Mulago Hill he was required to move out of his home to a smaller house in Kampala, because he would no longer be doing emergency surgery or need to live near the hospital. With Yusufu's help he worked hard to get it ready for when Olive arrived. From May 1964 until January 1966 Denis and Olive remained in Africa together.

During these last two years in Uganda Denis was able to put into practice schemes he had worked out during his last leave in Ireland. He planned to enlist the personal help of doctors in as many district hospitals as possible, both government and mission, throughout the three East African territories of Kenya, Uganda and Tanzania.

Doctors who agreed would be asked to fill in a monthly questionnaire that would enable Denis to put together a picture of how different forms of cancer and other diseases were distributed in these areas. He reckoned a monthly questionnaire with just a few questions would be best, because it could be filled in from memory — much less demanding than looking back at records. Each questionnaire Denis sent out was accompanied by a pre-addressed envelope, carrying a stamp of the country from which it was to be returned.

As an independent MRC worker with a free hand to study the distribution patterns of various forms of cancer in East Africa, Denis was able to travel widely, making personal contact with many of these doctors, their families and their medical staff. Without exception, he records a good welcome wherever he went. He had learned on previous safaris the value of offering to help individual doctors with any surgical problems they faced. Many of the men he met had been his students at Makerere.

During 1964 and 1965 he made eleven road safaris in East Africa, visiting most of the hospitals in these territories, up to four a day in the more densely populated areas. Each trip lasted for two to three weeks and covered distances of 1,000 to 2,000 miles, mostly over unmade roads.

To Denis this travel through the open expanse of the African countryside was always a joy — the familiar noises, sights and smells, the roadside picnics, the hot baths at the end of the day and the friendly evening conversations with new or renewed acquaintances. Denis was at his happiest when Olive could go with him. Together they were able to share experiences very different from those usually associated with the conventional concept of cancer research, with its focus on microscopes, test-tubes and animal experiments.

Two journeys were made by air. They took Denis on explorations of the Sudan, the largest country in Africa, covering an area of almost half a million square miles. At its capital, Khartoum, the White Nile from Uganda in the south and the Blue Nile from Ethiopia in the east meet, and then flow north through Egypt to the Mediterranean. For the most part he found the country very different from the sub-Saharan Africa he had been used to: different in climate, customs, vegetation, and in disease patterns.

During this time Denis began to receive invitations to undertake other forms of travel, to visit organizations in Western countries where scientific staff wanted to learn about the medical and epidemiological discoveries that were being made in Africa. The first of these was to Germany, to visit the makers of Endoxan (cyclophosphanide), one of the cancer-treating drugs he was using with success. He was also called to the World Health Organization in Geneva.

And in London he was asked to address the ear-nose-and-throat (oto-rhyno-laryngological) section of the Royal Society of Medicine. He felt something of an interloper in this specialist subject, as he spoke about his tumour in general with very little reference to ENT surgery. In his early days in Uganda he had done some ENT surgery because there was no one else to do it. But he did not enjoy it, neither had he acquired any real competence in it.

It was a big surprise therefore when, several months later, he heard that his presentation had been considered the best of the year and that he had been awarded the Society's Harrison Prize. It was the first of many prizes to be given him, prizes and awards which acknowledged not only his highly original and successful approaches to research, but also his ability to communicate his experiences in a forceful and amusing way.

From London he went to Dublin to lecture at his own medical school at Trinity College, then, after lecturing in Derby, he returned to Uganda via Amara and Addis Ababa.

In between trips like these and his overland safaris a lot of time was spent writing papers for scientific journals. In the school holidays, when the girls flew in from England, the office work at Mulago Hospital became something of a family affair, as all of them helped to analyze the records, construct charts and plot disease distribution on maps of East Africa.

Details concerning the distribution of different types of cancer in the three countries, as well as others, continued to flow in. Denis combined these with information obtained from central pathology labs in each of the countries to build up as complete a distribution-picture as possible. There were some remarkable differences in the distribution of different types of cancer, as two examples will show.

Cancer of the gullet (oesophagus) was found to be the commonest cancer in men in the western part of Kenya, particularly in the plains adjacent to the upper part of the east coast of Lake Victoria. It was also common in eastern Zimbabwe, southern Malawi and in the Pare mountains of Tanzania. Lower down the east coast of Lake Victoria, in north-west Tanzania, it was much less common. In the densely populated countries of Rwanda and Burundi not one case of this type of cancer could be found.

By contrast, cancer of the stomach was most commonly recorded in Rwanda and Burundi. The only other area recording high incidence for this cancer in East Africa was on the slopes of Mt Kilimanjaro, in northern Tanzania.

The reasons for these distinctive distribution patterns, and others like them, remained obscure. But in the years that followed they provided Denis with the incentive to expand on his work on the geography of cancer distribution.

They also provided him with graphic means of illustrating to doctors in the West how disease patterns can change over relatively short distances in developing countries. He hit on the idea of taking his audiences on an imaginary journey, following the course of the Nile. It began in the mountains of Burundi, at the source of the Kagera River, which flows into Lake Victoria to become in turn the Victoria Nile and the White Nile, until it joins the Blue Nile in Khartoum.

By this route, finishing up in the Mediterranean, he described the different diseases characteristic of the journey, using illustrations to show the various diseases, the changing scenery, the customs of the people and the topography of the country. It was a most unusual approach to medical lecturing and one that became immensely popular.

He was also able to show how, even in one country such as the Sudan, there could be great contrasts in disease patterns, greater than anywhere between southern Sudan and South Africa. And he gave the reasons. The people of the northern Sudan are Muslims who have moved south from North Africa, sharing a common culture, ethnic background and historical tradition with the people of the north. By contrast, the southern Sudanese are black Africans, living as peasant agriculturalists and, for Denis, these distinctions exposed the fallacy of assuming that disease distribution followed political frontiers.

Although his interest in disease distribution was growing, Denis still continued treating his lymphoma patients who were responding with increasing success to chemotherapy treatment. His diary records children turning up, after several years' absence, apparently completely cured. It also records details of his outside activities, the Bible studies and Sunday services in the large protectorate prison to which he and several of his medical colleagues were now deeply committed. Another of his concerns was the financial welfare of Mengo Mission Hospital.

Not surprisingly then when, in February 1966, the time finally came for the Burkitts to leave Uganda and return to England, there was much sadness both for them and for their many African friends, some of whom they had known for twenty years. And it was not only African friends they were leaving behind. As well as many European colleagues there was a whole community of Asian Christians whom the Burkitts had come to love.

During their years in Kampala they had supported the work of the Mission to Asians, at one time with Denis as secretary. A farewell tea party organized by this group of Asian Christians and held at All Saints' Church was a tearful occasion for everyone. Replying to the presentation and speeches by those they would be leaving behind for ever, Denis reminded them that 'we are all one in Christ Jesus; in him differences of colour and race cease to matter'.

For Denis such differences had long since ceased to matter, from that day when he brought home from college in Dublin the first black man to be seen in the streets of Enniskillen. There had been some prejudice and fear of the unknown, even in his own home, but as Denis realized in later life his meeting with Cofie George was one of the small but important beginnings from which his desire to serve the people of the great continent of Africa had sprung.

Now, after twenty years, that intimate contact with these people was to be severed. The saddest parting of all for Denis, Olive, Judy, Cass and Rachel was at Entebbe airport. There to see them off were many friends, including Yusufu, their faithful servant of twenty years and long since one of the family. The tears flowed. Would they ever meet again? As it happened, they did. But what eventually happened to Yusufu during the Amin reign of terror they never found out.

CHAPTER 13

'The Bran Man'

With his move to England Denis found the routine of his working life transformed. He was transported from the heat and humidity of tropical Africa, surrounded mostly by black faces and brightly-coloured dresses, to the overcoats and late winter greyness of London's West End. From the window at his Medical Research Council External Staff office he could watch the milling crowds and slow-moving traffic below, in Tottenham Court Road.

To commute daily on the London underground was about as big a shift in life-style as could be imagined. Not that Denis had any intention of becoming desk-bound. Neither would he let his new surroundings curtail his studies into cancer distribution in tropical Africa, and, increasingly, in other parts of the world. It was the policy of the MRC to take on people who had already proved themselves and then give them a free hand. So, before long, Denis was planning new adventures.

The 10,000-mile safari had already earned him a reputation for being economical in his use of other people's money. As a result he now found that any requests made to his new employers were met without question. He planned to undertake two trips a year to Africa and budgeted accordingly. The purpose was to collect information about cancer distribution. He regarded the people he visited in government and mission hospitals as experts in their own corners of the world, able to play a valuable role in his research.

Within six months of returning to England Denis was on his

way back to Africa for an intensive three-week tour. This visit
took him over much of the ground he had covered five years
earlier, on his long safari. It was a chance to meet many of his
old friends again, including his safari companion, Cliff Nelson,
and his wife Beth, still working together at their mission
hospital in Kola Ndota.

Then, on to a medical conference in Blantyre, during which
he and three other delegates spent half an hour in conversation
with the country's president, Dr Hastings Banda.

He also returned to Makerere University, where he had been
a lecturer at the Medical School. He met again Professor Pul-
verstaft, who had been one of the audience of twelve people
listening to his first lymphoma lecture in London and in
consequence was now living and working in Africa. 'To see his
dedication to the study of this tumour,' Denis wrote, 'demon-
strated to me that mere numbers are a poor index to the success
of a meeting.'

The day Denis arrived back from his Africa trip he picked up
the key of the family's first permanent home of their own in
England. It was the end of a long and frustrating period of
house-hunting, made harder by the fact that the only constraint
was the need to be within commuting distance of central
London. The search had taken them from Kent to Oxford,
from Essex to Berkshire. Finally they settled for the south-east
corner of Oxfordshire. On 16 August, almost twenty years to
the day since Denis had left Olive and his parents to go to
Uganda, they moved from their rented house in Nettlebed
to The Knoll in the village of Shiplake.

The next few months for Denis and Olive were busy, happy
ones. Always a do-it-yourself man and not wanting to spend
money wastefully, Denis was in his element: clearing out the
garage and the woodshed, building a bench for his heavy vice,
and putting up his drill rack. In the garden he struggled to
master an obstinate motor mower and cut back the yew hedge
with a newly-acquired trimmer.

Inside the house there were wardrobes to build, shelves and
mirrors to put up and the cellar to clear for use as a dark-room.
Together he and Olive laid carpets and assembled wall-lights.

Crates arrived from Uganda, Nettlebed and Laragh and with them came many memories from the past, as when Denis came across his father's old tool-chest with its contents of well-worn but lovingly cared-for tools.

Together, Olive and Denis visited local house auctions and acquired a very mixed collection of artefacts, dressers and chairs and tables, a settee, wheelbarrow, bicycle, a garden hose and lawn mower, a piano stool and chairs. All this Denis fitted in between commuting to London and writing scientific papers.

Then, in October 1966, he was off again, this time on his most ambitious tour yet. He had had three papers accepted for the UICC (Union International Contre le Cancer) conference to be held that year in Tokyo. A journey to such a far-away destination provided an opportunity to visit many other countries, either on the way out or on the way back. He spent time in Singapore, Ceylon, Hong Kong, New Zealand, New Guinea, Thailand, Pakistan and Iraq, at each place adding contacts to his expanding network and gathering further statistics on cancer distribution.

This self-imposed world-wide tour reminded him once again of his youthful voyage to Manchuria on the *Glen Shiel* during which the conviction had grown that God was calling him to work overseas in a third-world country, and of his time in Ceylon as a major in the Royal Army Medical Corps during the final months of the war. As his plane touched down in Colombo he recalled his time in the military hospital there. It had been in a requisitioned school near a sandy beach, south of the city. It was during that war-time period in Colombo that he had had that chance meeting with his brother Robin.

The meeting was one that Robin also remembers well.

'Towards the end of the war I was in the Far East with a beach medical unit of the 14th Army. On the way home for demobilization our ship stopped at Colombo for the afternoon. I knew Denis was stationed at a hospital near the city and thought I must try to contact him. It had been several years since we'd last met. I went ashore and rang the hospital, only to find that he had gone into the city for the day.'

Disappointed at being so close and yet missing his brother, Robin left the telephone and went into a nearby café for coffee and to decide what to do next. The first person he saw as he walked through the door was Denis. Six thousand miles from home the two brothers, who as boys had been such close companions but whose paths had since rarely crossed, were able to spend a few hours together before they again went their separate ways.

The most profitable part of Denis's 1966 Japanese trip was after the Tokyo conference, when he and his old friend George Oéttle went on a tour of New Guinea. It had been discovered five years earlier by an Australian scientist that this was one of the few countries outside Africa where Burkitt's lymphoma was endemic. As Denis Burkitt and George Oéttle travelled the island (which is twice the size of Britain) it was exciting to see first-hand how the distribution of the lymphoma was determined by exactly the same climatic conditions Denis had discovered in Africa. The lymphoma was rare in the mountains, and in the dry regions around Port Moresby in the south, and common along the moist and hot northern coast and the off-shore islands.

With George Oéttle's help as a pathologist and epidemiologist, Denis was able to gather a mass of information about other forms of cancer too, some of them more closely associated with factors of custom and culture than with climate. He saw first-hand how, as in India, the habit of chewing a concoction of betel nut and lime coincided with cancer of the cheek.

From Port Moresby the two friends travelled together as far as Brisbane. Here Denis had arranged to talk with local cancer workers before flying on to several other Australian cities, then to Bangkok, Karachi, Baghdad and home. It was the last time he was to see his friend alive. George Oéttle died two years later, after a heart operation. In determining to track down the distribution and cause of his lymphoma Denis had owed much to this man who, back in 1957, had stated so categorically that 'this tumour does not occur in South Africa', and so started him wondering if there was a lymphoma boundary.

In his book called *The Long Safari*, which tells the story of the
lymphoma and the discovery of its cause, the American medical
writer Bernard Glemser records this tribute to Oéttle by a
colleague and well-known cancer researcher, Professor James
Murray:

'Critical to a degree, he used his brilliant mind to test and
evaluate every statement he encountered and every set of facts
uncovered in the course of his research. Nothing irritated him
more than loose or slovenly thinking, and he delighted in the
application of logic to the assessment of his research findings
. . . He had a profound knowledge of the Bible and was a man of
deep and unshakable faith in the Providence of God. Despite
his brilliant mind, his great scientific achievements, and his
research ability he was a humble and lovable man . . . No one
could be long in the presence of George Oéttle without
realizing that this was a man whose every thought and action
was coloured and determined by Christian love and faith.'

Back home in England, after his seven-week world tour,
Denis settled down to analyze the mountains of information he
had gathered. He was now fifty-six, an internationally-known
figure in the world of cancer research, equally popular on the
conference platform and in the hospital wards. God willing, he
could expect to look forward to another decade or so of quietly
collecting and analyzing data sent from around the world
relating to cancer distribution, combining daily commuting to
his London office with the occasional fact-finding visit or
lecture tour abroad.

He and Olive were looking forward to sharing the pleasure of
their new home together, with their family and friends. Indeed
many people did stay with them in the years that followed.
Some years over 100 guests recorded their stay in the Burkitts'
visitors' book. They also watched their daughters grow into
young women, become engaged and be married in the village
church at Shiplake. Wedding receptions for all three were held
in marquees on the lawn at The Knoll.

But the future for Denis was in many ways to be very
different from what he imagined, or from what Olive might
have wished. In *The Long Safari* Glemser stated his opinion

that following the discoveries relating to the lymphoma the Burkitt story was 'still only half told, there will be more to come'. These were prophetic words. As the Burkitts entered 1967 Denis's medical career was about to take off in a totally new and unexpected direction.

It began with a phone call from Dr (later Sir) Richard Doll, the Director of the Medical Research Council's Statistical Unit, who had an office a few blocks away from Denis.

'I have a man here I think you might be interested in meeting. Statistically I could pull much of his work to pieces, but nonetheless I have a hunch his ideas may be right.'

It was another prophetic statement — about a man Denis had then not heard of, but whom he was to get to know very well. The man in question was a retired naval physician, Captain T. L. (Peter) Cleave. He was a man with some very unorthodox views on the relationship between diet and Western diseases, views which were treated with great scepticism by the medical profession at the time. Subsequently he was acknowledged to be one of the major pioneers of what became known as the 'fibre hypothesis'.

In the early pages of his international bestselling book, *Don't forget fibre in your diet*, Denis Burkitt has this to say about Cleave:

'One of the first to recognize a relationship between refined carbohydrate foods and disease was Dr T. R. Allinson who, in an essay written nearly a century ago, related not only constipation but also piles (haemorrhoids) and varicose veins to an insufficiency of fibre in the diet. Sir Robert MacCarrison, early in the 1900s, warned of the dangers of over-processed food.

'These observations did not receive serious attention until Surgeon Captain T. L. Cleave, a British naval physician with perceptive genius, persuasive argument and irrefutable logic, not only linked together a number of diseases of unknown cause but presented compelling evidence that each of them might be only a different result of a common cause — the consumption of over-refined carbohydrate foods.

'Captain Cleave was also the first to demonstrate dramatically the beneficial effect of bran in combating constipation when he was chief medical officer responsible for the health of the crew of the battleship *King George V* during the Second World War. It was he who first persuaded me of the profound influence of diet on patterns of disease.

'Meeting Captain Cleave was one of the most important occasions in my professional life. Background knowledge of disease patterns in the third world enabled me to recognize instantly the undeniable truth and logic of his ideas. I also had unique opportunities through medical contacts in much of Africa and Asia to confirm or deny statements he had made, and . . . the mass of opinion endorsed his conclusions. Most of the medical profession at that time viewed Captain Cleave's ideas with scepticism and consequently his evidence was rejected without proper consideration.'

Denis Burkitt had never been one to reject any serious ideas without proper consideration. So, after their first meeting in his MRC office, the two men were to have many 'fruitful encounters', as Denis called them. They did not always agree, but clearly they had much in common. Denis found Cleave to have an intensely enquiring mind, combined with the courage to challenge conventional concepts which, although long cherished, may never have been subjected to careful scrutiny.

In particular they had in common an ability to visualize apparently diverse diseases as possibly having a common cause. In Denis Burkitt's case it had been tumours growing in different parts of the body which were one type of lymphoma. For Cleave the list of diseases was vastly more diverse. It included many of major importance and high frequency — coronary heart disease, gall-stones, piles, appendicitis, diverticular disease of the colon, diabetes, varicose veins and many others.

Cleave was convinced that these diseases were the result of over-refined food and a lack of fibre. His conviction was not just a theoretical one. It was based on practical experience beginning in the confines of a battleship carrying 1,500 men during the Second World War. On board *King George V* he became popular when he dispensed raw bran to the crew, having first tried it on himself. To many it brought relief from an almost universal complaint — constipation.

In view of the widespread acceptance of the bran theory today, it is hard to appreciate just how novel such treatment was in the 1940s. Bran had probably not been used in that way in such large quantities before. Soon Cleave was using it to treat related problems such as piles. As a result of his success he became known in the navy as the 'bran man' — not always to his advantage.

An American book records the beginnings of the fibre story in *The truth about fibre in your diet*. Referring to those early days its author, Lawrence Galton, writes that Cleave was 'sometimes the object of ridicule as word got around that with him bran was a panacea and that he was inordinately fond of bananas'. Galton tells how Cleave's wife Helen recalls that even many years later she would repeatedly meet an old acquaintance at the naval club and at parties who would greet her with a 'Hello Helen, are you still living on bran and bananas?'

'Sometimes,' Helen Cleave says, 'I used to feel quite huffy and would tell them we had very good food. Come to lunch and you will have more than bran and bananas.'

Concerning Cleave's ideas Galton comments that 'even if they were not to be accepted in full, they should have triggered some interest in all the years he had been trying to be heard. But they didn't; for all intents and purposes he was in limbo. A concept of a single causative factor operating in many varied diseases not commonly considered to have anything to do with each other — a hypothesis that these seemingly distinct and separate diseases are really the same disease manifesting itself in many body systems — was difficult to accept.'

Although Denis Burkitt could not accept the concept of a single disease he could and did accept the idea of a common cause. But he knew what it was like to find his ideas of a common cause initially unacceptable. For him, acceptance had come only after he had established the link by sheer hard work and singleminded determination, with the co-operation of other medical scientists.

Now it was Denis's turn to provide the co-operation. As he

listened he began to realize that the diseases Cleave was talking about *were* rare in those areas of the world with which he was most familiar — the third-world countries where the supposed 'benefits' of refined food had not yet reached the ordinary people.

He felt great sympathy as he heard of the man's efforts to get his views more widely known, mainly through booklets he had published initially at his own expense, and through letters to medical journals. It reminded him of the poor response to his first paper on jaw tumours when it appeared in the *British Journal of Surgery*. Like Denis, Cleave too was convinced of the truth of what he was saying, but until now hardly anyone else was. Denis Burkitt was to change all that.

He had one asset which had been denied Cleave but which he could now use to get him a wider audience. Denis Burkitt's reputation gained in the field of cancer research had given him a platform. It gave him an attentive audience and enabled him to speak when others would not have had a hearing. Had there been no Burkitt's lymphoma, no matter how inspired Denis might have been by Cleave's hypothesis, he would have been considered just another food crank. But no one dared to think so by this time.

CHAPTER 14

The Saccharine Disease

Denis Burkitt's first task was to find out more about this controversial man Cleave and to discover what lay behind his refined carbohydrate hypothesis. He knew intuitively from his third-world experiences that the man was fundamentally right, but for Denis that was not enough. He began by reading all the leaflets and books Cleave had written. And the two men met a number of times in Denis's office.

He learned of Cleave's own wartime experiences. He also heard of other wartime stories Cleave had come across. There was, for instance, the case of the German soldiers fighting outside Leningrad, and living through the severe winter months on any coarse food they could find. German medical records showed that fewer of those troops suffered from peptic ulcers than those living on better food behind the battle zone.

This discovery, which appeared to contradict the general view that ulcers were caused by stress, was put down to the fact that the soldiers were being forced to forage for themselves and were eating raw vegetables and sour-bread. After capture they continued on unrefined food with no ill effect. Only when they got back home at the end of the war did those who had previously suffered from ulcers have a relapse.

After the war, Cleave began in earnest to make a study of human eating habits. He discovered that for thousands of years people had eaten a diet of minimally-processed food, with only occasional meat. Artificial concentrations of sugar were absent from the diet to which human beings had adapted over a long period of time. But in the last 200 years all that had changed, as the Western world had developed economically and food had become 'refined'.

From these findings Cleave was driven to the conclusion that the human body had been unable to adapt to these relatively sudden changes. It was incapable of handling the energy released so quickly into the bloodstream from the concentrated sugar and white flour.

The problem was compounded by a lack of fibre in refined food, which meant that the bowels were not working efficiently. With the eye of a visionary, Cleave became convinced that this two-fold disorder was at the root of many of the non-infective diseases which, with the eradication of so many infective diseases, now dominated the medical problems of the Western world.

He compiled a list of such diseases. It included coronary heart disease, the commonest cause of death in the West; gallstones, the most frequent cause of abdominal surgery; appendicitis, the commonest abdominal emergency operation; diverticular disease — pouches in the colon — one of the commonest disorders of the intestine; as well as diabetes, varicose veins and haemorrhoids, obesity, dental caries and peptic ulcers.

Cleave was in fact arguing that these were not separate diseases at all but different manifestations of a single disease which he labelled 'The Saccharine Disease'. Here he was using the word saccharine to mean 'related to sugar', not the chemical sweetener of that name. What had promoted the occurrence of these diseases was the development of food-processing machinery which could remove fibre from flour on the one hand and produce convenient and tasty, sugar-rich products on the other.

His first serious attempt to make his hypothesis public was in 1955 when he wrote an article for the *Journal of the Royal Navy Medical Service*. Like Denis Burkitt's first article on the distribution of his tumour, it attracted minimal attention — again it was in the wrong journal and it was too early. Added to which, Cleave was almost unknown outside the Royal Naval Hospital in Gosport, where he was then working.

Among his colleagues the little attention it did attract resulted mostly in ridicule. What a contrast, twenty-three years
later, when at the same hospital Cleave, then seventy-two, was
presented with the Gilbert Blane Gold Medal for Naval
Medicine and the Harben Gold Medal of the Royal Institute of
Public Health by the Navy's Medical Director, Vice-Admiral
Sir John Rawlins. Only then was the importance of his pioneer
work publicly recognized. His name was added to the long list
of eminent recipients of the Harben Medal which included
Pasteur, Lister and Fleming.

Having failed to attract serious attention for his hypothesis,
Cleave set out to gather further evidence in support of it. He
wrote by hand several thousand letters (no one is sure how
many) to doctors around the world, from the affluent West to
the rural and tribal East.

From the replies he received to questions concerning diseases
treated or observed, he was able to build up a picture showing
the emergence of certain non-infective diseases and their geographical and socio-economic distribution.

He analyzed the data and began publishing a series of books
setting out his findings. Then, in 1966, after retiring from the
Royal Navy, he put all his findings together in one book:
Diabetes, Coronary Thrombosis and the Saccharine Disease. Although it was written with the help of Dr George Campbell, a
diabetes expert living in Durban, in South Africa, the essential
thesis of the book was Cleave's alone.

It was this book in particular which impressed Denis Burkitt.

'In it,' he said, 'I found a logical, coherent and persuasive
argument that the associations observed between the diseases
and their distribution could only be satisfactorily explained by
a common causative factor.

'Here again was the same kind of reasoning that had persuaded me ten years previously that many tumours hitherto
considered to be totally different conditions must in fact all be
part of a single disease.

'Cleave's clear thinking and courageous challenging of
conventionally accepted but obviously untenable medical
concepts immensely appealed to me. It had always been in my

nature to question the reasons behind things that were done because they had always been done.'

Weight was added to Cleave's arguments by Denis's own observations in the UK and abroad. Soon after his first meeting with Cleave, Denis went on one of his increasingly frequent trips to America. As he toured the hospital wards between lectures and press interviews he became acutely aware that a large proportion of the patients he saw were suffering from complaints virtually unknown in the parts of Africa with which he was familiar.

Cleave had laid great stress in his writings on the fact that these Western diseases were now as common amongst black as amongst white Americans. Since the ancestors of the black Americans came from Africa, Cleave drew the conclusion that the diseases must be caused by environmental rather than by genetic factors.

Now Denis was seeing first-hand in American hospitals the evidence of this.

'I quickly realized the enormous importance of what Cleave was saying and became convinced of the truth of what Sir Richard Doll, who had first introduced me to Cleave, had written in the introduction to the second edition of Cleave's book.'

Doll had said: 'Whether the predictions that Surgeon Captain Cleave and Dr Campbell make in this book will prove to be correct remains to be seen; but if only a small part of them do then the authors will have made a bigger contribution to medicine than most university departments or medical research units make in the course of a generation.'

Today most of the fundamental assertions made by Cleave in his book have been substantiated, if not definitely proved, by the geographical and medical evidence. The emphasis has moved away from excess of sugar to a deficiency in fibre, but the concept that refined carbohydrate food is dangerous to health is now almost universally accepted.

Denis likened Cleave's work to that of an explorer of new lands:

'No notable explorer has ever made initial maps that were

not subsequently improved on by those with better facilities. Cleave's theories have been modified as knowledge has increased. But the process underlines rather than detracts from the greatness of Cleave's pioneer work of discovery.

'Where Cleave's hypothesis was particularly brilliant was that it included the two complementary components of the effects of refining carbohydrate foods. These are on the one hand the over-consumption of sugar, which is extracted in a concentrated or fibre-free form from cane or beet, and on the other the removal from food of fibre which is an essential element of diet for the maintenance of health.'

Regrettably Cleave would never accept that fat could play a contributory role in the causation of disease, arguing that it had always been a component of the human diet. The crucial factor is, of course, that someone in the West today consumes more than three times the proportion of his energy from fat than his counterpart in the rural populations of the third world.

From all he heard, read and saw, Denis became increasingly committed to discovering for himself the exact nature of the relationship between refined foods and disease. It would not be an easy task. He was to find vested interests amongst medical experts and food manufacturers, who initially did not take kindly to the implications of what he was now setting out to do.

As he researched back into medical history, Denis soon discovered that Cleave was not the first medical man to be labelled a quack for his dietary ideas. A hundred years before, Dr Allinson had been struck off the medical register for malpractice because he had recommended and sold wholemeal bread. The plate outside his Harley Street consulting-rooms read: Dr T. R. Allinson, *ex*-MRCP.

In 1880 Allinson had written:

'One great curse of this country is constipation of the bowel which is caused in great measure by white bread. From this constipation come piles, varicose veins, headaches, miserable feelings, dullness and other ailments. Separating the bran from the flour may be said to have come into fashion at the beginning of this (the nineteenth) century and as a consequence pill factories are now an almost necessary part of the State.'

Delving further back into history, Denis found that Hippocrates, the father of modern medicine in the third century BC, and the Persian physician Hakim in the ninth century AD had both extolled the bowel-emptying virtues of coarse flour and bran.

As Denis pondered these findings and studied the work of Cleave he began to see the potential they held for preventing non-infectious diseases on a massive scale through changes in diet. Moreover, he realized that with his past experience of geographical pathology he was in a unique position to field-test, and hopefully confirm, the connection between refined food and diseases.

'I had had over twenty years' medical experience in third-world countries; not only in Uganda, but previously amongst East African and Indian troops in Kenya and Ceylon during the war. And now working for the Medical Research Council in London I was receiving monthly reports from some 140 mainly rural hospitals in Africa, plus a few in India, mostly mission hospitals run by dedicated staff with many years' experience in one place.'

The information network had been built up over the years for collecting data on patients with cancer. Now it would prove the ideal means of finding out to what extent Western diseases had begun to emerge in rural and tribal areas of the underdeveloped and developing world.

Much later Denis was able to use the same network to test a theory that Western disease emerged, or became common, in a community in a given sequence. He found it true to a surprising degree.

Early in 1969 Denis prepared a summary of Cleave's work. He used this as a basis for a questionnaire in which he asked doctors and hospital staff if they had seen any of the diseases listed by Cleave. He also took advantage of an opportunity greatly to extend his information-gathering network to bring into it many other areas of the third world. It involved using an already-existing network for the distribution of drugs to mission stations.

This particular story had begun a decade earlier when Ray

Knighton, from America, visited the Burkitts' home in Mulago. Like Denis, Ray was an active Christian. And the two men became immediate friends. They met again on Denis's subsequent lecture visits to North America. On his way to a cancer conference in Houston in 1968 Denis stopped off at the offices of Ray Knighton in Chicago, where he ran the Medical Assistance Program.

Knighton had started MAP out of his concern for the medical needs of the poorer nations. Shrewdly he had recognized the potential opportunity to meet those needs in the fact that all drug companies and makers of medical equipment in North America had excess stock at some time. To store these cost money. Often they would be overtaken in the market by improved products with greater appeal to the public. To throw away obsolete products or out-of-date drugs meant a total loss for the companies concerned.

But if supplies could be donated to third-world countries through a registered charity, the tax laws were such that the drug or equipment company could at least recover tax. Knowing this, Knighton approached companies all over North America and found many only too happy to supply the goods that were taking up valuable space. Most were prepared to deliver them free of charge to the MAP warehouses near Chicago. Some even made financial donations. In exchange they had a receipt from Ray Knighton for the tax-man.

By the time Denis visited the MAP offices in Chicago in 1968 the organization had become one of America's largest charities, serving mission hospitals throughout the world. Over 1,000 mission hospitals were being regularly circulated with lists of available drugs and equipment. All the doctor had to do was to fill in an order form. MAP was even beginning to send out food and voluntary manpower, and take a leading role in providing relief for disasters.

Since doctors in the field were receiving such generous donations, they could hardly object to filling in a simple questionnaire sent out with each list of available items — or so Denis argued. His friend in Chicago agreed. Denis prepared a questionnaire which asked to what extent the diseases listed had been seen at the mission hospital or in the surrounding district.

With all his questionnaires Denis was careful to encourage accurate reporting. It was important to know where possible the exact location of any diseases seen, together with precise details of a patient's age, sex and occupation. He had learned from his lymphoma-plotting days that details like these contained the clues to the answers he was seeking.

All through 1968 and 1969 a mass of valuable information from all over the third world came across the desk in Denis's London office. Much of it came from places where, without the help of MAP, the questionnaires would have ended up in some jungle waste-bin. Time and again they brought confirmation that the diseases listed by Cleave were found only in situations where Western civilization, along with Western diet and refined foods, was beginning to have its influence.

The exceptions were in themselves a confirmation. It was revealed that on the one hand there were within the third-world countries isolated instances of communities where the influence of Western culture (the discovery perhaps of a valuable mineral or fuel) had been followed by a rapid growth in some typically Western disease. Equally there were communities in the West which had to a marked extent escaped the ill-effects of economic development.

Over the years that followed Denis was able to visit many of these places. He travelled to Loma Linda in California to meet the non-drinking, non-smoking, largely vegetarian Seventh-Day Adventists; and to Salt Lake City to visit the beef-loving but non-smoking and mostly teetotal Mormons. He went to Arizona to meet the Pima Indians, whose rapid introduction to Western diet had resulted in them (unlike any other Indian tribe) having the highest gall-stone and the second highest diabetic rates in the world. He visited hospitals in Alaska and Alberta catering for the Eskimos.

In Australia he learned about the Aborigines and in New Zealand met with the Maori people. Through other doctors he met on his travels he discovered the extent to which life on individual Polynesian islands, many thousands of miles apart from their neighbours, could differ. Whereas on one island people were still dependent on traditional foods, those on others had developed a taste for the delights of cola drinks and white bread.

From the time he met Cleave in 1967 Denis increasingly took advantage of his safaris abroad as part of his cancer research for the MRC to persuade doctors and mission hospital staff to carry out their own local surveys of disease amongst selected groups or tribes of people. His ability to persuade already busy people to do such work was put down, by those who knew him well enough to tease him, to the fact that he had kissed the Blarney stone as a boy.

Denis's own description of the persuasion process was rather more matter-of-fact.

'When visiting a lonely mission hospital in the middle of Africa, you say to the only doctor in the region: "Do you realize, Dr Smith, that you are a world authority?" Taken aback, he replies: "Don't fool me. How can I be an authority on anything here, isolated as I am from any professional contact and with the minimum facilities?"

'To this you reply: "Have you considered that no one else in the world knows more about the pattern of disease distribution in the tribes you work with than you do?" The response this usually evokes is something like: "Come to think of it, you might be right."

'Your doctor then wants to know what he can do, and to his further surprise you suggest that he takes a note-book and records evidences of diseases he *doesn't* see. It invariably inspires a new interest in his work and before long there may be a short article appearing in that country's own medical journal.'

The result of all Denis's efforts and persuasion was a mass of geographical evidence which proved, to his satisfaction at least, that the distribution of the diseases which Cleave listed, along with a few other diseases, coincided with Westernization and the refinement of food which went with it. He was now convinced that changes in life-style and in diet had major roles to play in their cause.

The hypothesis was consistent with the geographical distribution of the diseases and with the emigration of communities from low-disease areas to high-disease areas. It was consistent with the life-styles of individual communities such as the Seventh-Day Adventists within Western society. And it was consistent with the historical emergence of the diseases, most of which were rare or unknown before the end of the nineteenth century.

But there was more to substantiate Cleave's hypothesis than making a connection between diet and disease. One of his fundamental tenets was that a person's risk of developing many of the common Western diseases was directly related to the contents of the intestines and the effect that had on bowel behaviour.

From his discussions with doctors in London hospitals and his search through medical textbooks Denis became aware that this was a subject about which the medical profession was woefully ignorant. He did eventually discover others who had done work on this taboo subject but they had largely been ignored.

For the present it was up to him. Towards the middle of 1969, to use his own words, he 'threw discretion to the wind' and began his own first-hand experiments into stool charac-teristics and bowel behaviour. He did it with as much enthusiasm as he had carried out his studies into lymphoma distribution. And his first guinea-pigs were the members of his own family.

CHAPTER 15

Fibre in the Diet

Denis Burkitt's diary entry for 4 July 1969 reads simply: 'Finished bowel transit tests on family. Pleased with results.'

As time went by he was to get increasing pleasure from the results of similar tests carried out amongst natives in Africa and public school boys in England. The results were to prove extremely important in highlighting fibre deficiency as a major cause of disease.

Following the experiments on his family's bowel behaviour, the next relevant event happened eight weeks later when, in Johannesburg at the end of August, he met Dr Alec Walker for the first time. Denis had gone to South Africa, after a visit to Uganda, to meet Dr George Campbell, who had contributed to Cleave's book as an expert on diabetes and who lived in Durban.

Ironically, Campbell's grandfather had been largely responsible for making sugar a major export of Natal. Now convinced, like Cleave, that it was a major health hazard, he spent much of his time trying to persuade people it was bad for them.

Denis profited greatly from his discussions with Campbell and learned a lot about diet and diabetes. But infinitely more valuable was his meeting with Walker, who worked at the South African Institute of Medical Research, where he was head of the department of human biology. It began as a casual invitation back to tea at Walker's house, after Denis had spent the day lecturing at the Institute. And it developed into an ongoing friendship.

Not only did the two find that they shared a common faith.

What Denis learned of Walker's methodical dietary research amongst the various ethnic groups in and around Johannesburg and throughout South Africa was to be an inspiration to his own work.

Walker was a Scot who had trained in Britain as a biochemist before emigrating to South Africa in 1938. His involvement in the study of bowel behaviour and the nature and weight of stools began during the Second World War when South Africa, like Britain, was short of wheat. The natural thing to do was to change the national diet from white to brown bread, with less bran extracted from the wheat to make it go further.

This had already been done in Britain, where only 15 per cent of the bran was being removed instead of the pre-war 25 to 30 per cent. But in South Africa there was talk of extracting even less, perhaps none at all. In Britain it had been thought necessary to add calcium to the bread because it was feared that, with less bran being removed, less calcium from the wheat was being absorbed by the body.

For the South African government, planning to extract even less bran, this raised the question of how much calcium should be added. As a leading research worker in nutrition Alec Walker was given the job of carrying out calcium balance studies on black and white people in Africa, fed first with white bread and then with brown bread. It involved comparing food intake with waste and water output.

In his book, *The truth about fibre in your diet*, medical writer Lawrence Galton explains what happened then:

'Walker did the studies, many of them on African prisoners. He himself was one of the white subjects. He found that with a switch from white to brown bread, there were losses of calcium over the first month or so but then the losses became less and less. And not only was a balance reached, but soon there were gains in calcium level. Given time, the body adapted to brown bread . . .

'It was in the course of these studies that Walker became intrigued by the evident differences in the bowel behaviour of white people on the usual refined diet and the African prisoners who customarily received in prison their native high-fibre diet.'

Galton goes on to explain how one of the first things Walker noticed was that stool weight amongst Africans was commonly three times higher than stool weight amongst whites. By using coloured dyes swallowed in pills he also discovered that the food residue passed through the African people much more rapidly than through whites.

Walker enquired further. He learned from prison doctors that African prisoners suffered less from constipation. Appendicitis amongst them was rare. Moreover he found that white prisoners whose diet had been changed to one with more brown bread and less fat, sugar and meat were also less likely to develop appendicitis or suffer from constipation. There were even some diabetic prisoners who needed less insulin, or could go without.

During his time in Johannesburg Denis spent several hours with Walker. He saw the way he had tabulated his results. He learned how he had studied the behaviour of different ethnic groups — Indians, Africans, Whites and Coloureds — all living in the same climate in the same part of the world. They each had a totally different way of life, different foods, *and* different disease patterns.

Alec told Denis how, out of 10,000 black Africans eating traditional foods, he found only twenty-seven cases of appendicitis. If the disease had been as common as amongst white people it would have been nearer 850. In rural areas gall-stones were rare and few black people got fat, or suffered from diabetes.

Only as the black Bantu people became urbanized, moving into the black townships surrounding the big cities (like Soweto near Johannesburg) did they start to suffer Western diseases. Then traditional diets of mealie meal gave way to white bread and cola drinks.

Denis later commented: 'Once you'd met Alec Walker you could not help but be convinced. He wasn't content to study half-a-dozen different stools, or measure the transit time of a few people. He carried out thousands of tests, analyzed the results and got the facts. The man who can put down massive evidence like that wins the day in the end.'

Walker was not the only person Denis met in Africa who had made a scientific study of bowel behaviour. Nor, indeed, had his research been the first. Denis discovered this when, five months after his meeting with Alec Walker, on his next trip to Uganda he walked into the laboratory of Mengo Mission Hospital. He had gone there to weigh a collection of stools from a distant tribe in a primitive area.

He found Dr Ted Dimock at the lab. bench, carrying out a blood count. The doctor was helping out at Mengo during a vacation from his country practice in England, as he had done so often in mission hospitals around the world. He knew of Denis's interest in diet and disease and that on this trip he was studying bowel behaviour.

Dimock surprised Denis by telling him that it was a subject he had been very familiar with at one time. As far back as 1936 he had written a thesis on the effect of bran on bowel behaviour. It had involved weighing stool samples collected from patients in Britain suffering from constipation and piles, and then treating the patients with bran.

In those early days he had already discovered what Denis and Alec Walker now also knew that, with the use of bran, stools got bigger, heavier and softer and could be passed more easily.

His thesis was not well received. It did no more than gain Dimock his MD. Then for three decades it gathered dust. But when Denis later had a chance to read it, in combination with the work of Walker, it provided him with the inspiration to continue with his own experiments in bowel behaviour.

Alec Walker had used red dye pellets to determine transit times. But Denis found this method not accurate enough to measure the precise time-lapse between eating a meal and getting rid of the unabsorbed parts of the food. Instead he adapted the method of another worker and got his patients to swallow a number of plastic pellets the size of rice grains. These were impregnated with barium, to make them opaque to X-rays.

By X-raying the collected stools and counting the number of pellets it was possible to determine transit times more accurately.

This method presented some problems in remote areas of Africa, where no X-ray equipment was available. One time Denis drove 300 miles from a primitive part of the country to reach a hospital with X-ray equipment, his car loaded with bagged-up stools from the Karamajong tribe. Who would have believed that the contents of his car were required for serious medical research? But he enjoyed it all immensely, as his diary entry for that particular day shows: 'It was lots of fun and interest.'

The lack of other facilities in Africa, such as proper toilets, proved to be a positive advantage. With his keen eye and single-minded interest, a walk through the African bush could yield much useful information. More than once on a walk some leg-pulling companion took delight in photographing him taking close-up pictures of some dusty patch of ground and its rapidly drying contents. But he was not easily distracted. He knew that such close-ups would be very useful later, as he lectured to medical colleagues throughout the world.

Getting samples from people in Western countries was an infinitely more difficult task. It required 'every talent of per-suasion that could be mustered to get people even to preserve their stools'. Denis recalls the heroic efforts required to collect specimens from boys in an English public school.

'After a lecture on food and health I managed to enlist the help of thirty volunteers, who promised to swallow the pellets provided, and pass their stools into plastic bags. They were to write their name and the time passed on labels and then deposit the bags in the school laboratory. Twenty boys eventually complied.

'I personally weighed the bags each morning during the next five days and carried them with me by train to London to be X-rayed in a hospital adjacent to my office.'

The results of much of Denis's work, combined with that of Alec Walker's extensive research in South Africa and that of other British colleagues whom Denis had persuaded to help, were published in *The Lancet* in 1972 and in the *Journal of the American Medical Association* in 1973. These papers detailed the South African studies, which had shown that the average daily stool weights for the adult black in rural populations where there was minimum risk of developing Western diseases, were between 300 and 500 grams, with transit times of around thirty hours.

The weights for whites were around 100 to 150 grams, with transit times of about seventy hours. The results in Britain tallied closely with the white people of South Africa, with daily stool weights of 80 to 120 grams and transit times of around seventy-two hours.

By means of such statistics, the article brought to the attention of the medical world in a forceful way some fundamental differences in bowel behaviour between different groups living on different diets.

When speaking to medical audiences Denis began taking advantage of these occasions to bring into the open this still-taboo subject. To break his audience in gently, without causing too much offence, he usually began with some reference to history. A slide would be projected on the screen as he spoke. It would contain words which Lord Byron had scribbled on the lavatory wall at his home, Newstead Abbey, near Nottingham.

> 'O Cloacina Goddess of this place,
> Look on thy suppliant with smiling face.
> Soft and obedient may his motions flow
> Not rashly swift or obstinately slow.'

This slide would be followed by another, showing paragraphs from a book published in Dublin in 1733, dealing specifically with the subject of 'human ordure' (stools). It was the first essay of its kind ever published. With great enthusiasm the author had classified stools observed in the fields and villages around Dublin much as a botanist would classify plants, describing five types in picturesque detail. The author of this old book had given his name on the title page discreetly as Dr S . . .T. The subject was as taboo in the eighteenth century as it is today.

When he first acquired the book, Denis took it to an antiquarian bookseller in Edinburgh, who found reference to it in an old catalogue. The writer was none other than Dean

Jonathan Swift, author of *Gulliver's Travels* and a graduate of Denis's old university, Trinity College, Dublin.

Using anecdotes such as these, Denis was able to introduce his audience to this delicate subject with a light touch, while at the same time showing that there had been famous men in the past who had taken the subject seriously. His message was that his audience should do the same.

In 1969, two years after his first meeting with Cleave, Denis made his first visit to South America to address a cancer congress in Sao Paulo, organized by the American Cancer Society. It had been this Society's journal, *Cancer*, which had published Denis's first successful lymphoma paper, creating such excitement by revealing to an American audience the existence of a human cancer that could be related to environment. History was shortly to repeat itself.

At the congress Denis met Dr Roald Grant, one of the organizers. During an interview for a feature later published in a cancer journal, Denis revealed that as a result of his world-wide information network he believed he had substantiated Alec Walker's largely ignored suggestion that fibre could provide protection against bowel cancer.

He explained how the statistics showed that the distribution of bowel cancer throughout the world was identical to that of diverticular disease, against which, it was believed by then, adequate fibre in the diet could provide protection. It was an intriguing possibility that was not lost on Grant. Bowel cancer was, and still is, the number two cause of cancer death in North America and Western Europe after lung cancer.

Grant immediately invited Denis to prepare a paper on the subject for presentation at another major cancer conference the Society was arranging to take place the following year, in San Diego, California.

Regrettably, Grant died before the conference took place. But Denis went ahead, spending much time on his paper in which he outlined the world-wide geographical distribution of bowel cancer. Taking his lead from the work Alec Walker had done, he developed in his paper the hypothesis that the deficiency of fibre in Western diet was the major factor responsible for the high prevalence of this disease in more affluent societies.

The American medical press was immediately taken up with the concept that so-called 'roughage' could give protection against this fearful disease. In contrast, the conservative medical profession was, on the whole, sceptical.

Then, as now, the generally held view amongst cancer researchers was that diet was the most likely environmental factor responsible for bowel cancer. But they believed that fat in the diet was the prime suspect, with animal protein also being a candidate for suspicion. Any suggestion that fibre might play a role was thought unworthy of serious consideration.

Denis's paper, given at the conference under the title 'Epidemiology of cancer of the colon and rectum', was published the following year in *Cancer*. It took a long while for its message to sink in to the minds of the medical profession and cancer research workers but over the next ten years, as the role of fibre began to receive increasing attention, it became one of the papers most frequently referred to by other workers when discussing their own findings, with the result that in 1980, ten years after its publication, it became a 'citation classic' on the subject of bowel cancer.

Its acceptance as a 'citation classic' in 1980 gave Denis the opportunity to bring it up-to-date, for the benefit of the journal which publishes summaries of such papers. He also took advantage of the opportunity to correct what he regarded as the erroneous notion that he had been the first to implicate fibre deficiency with bowel cancer. Although he had been the first to write a definitive paper on the subject, he made it clear that the credit for originality should have gone to his friend Alec Walker.

Denis's first paper on the tumour that became known as Burkitt's lymphoma also became a citation classic. Not many men have achieved this distinction in two entirely unrelated fields of medical research.

Denis was not the only medical research worker concerned with diet and disease who had to acknowledge his debt to Alec

Walker. He discovered this when, in March 1970 (eight months after his meeting with Walker), he again met his old friend Hugh Trowell. They had met very occasionally since Denis had returned to England. But their 1970 meeting in Uganda was to prove of special importance to them both.

For Denis, its importance was the discovery that Hugh had also made some significant observations relating to his own interest in diet and disease and that in making them he had been influenced by what he had learned from Walker.

The occasion of the meeting between Denis and Hugh was the centenary celebrations of the birth of Sir Albert Cook, the missionary doctor who had founded Mengo Mission Hospital in Uganda at the end of the last century. Hugh Trowell, who was just retiring after ten years as parson of a country church in Wiltshire, had been invited by the Ugandan government to attend the celebrations. Trowell had nursed and cared for Sir Albert during his last days.

The main purpose of Denis's return to Uganda, with Olive, was to receive an honorary Doctor of Science degree from Makerere University. He had been lecturer in surgery at the medical school there from 1948 to 1964. At the award ceremony Denis was expected to give the closing address. But first some 600 students of the university had to receive their awards. He records that 'the meeting was held in the open and it was nearly dark by the time my turn came. There was barely enough light for me to read the notes for my closing remarks.'

The Ugandan Medical Association had planned this conference to coincide with the degree-conferring ceremony. Denis had been asked to be one of the lecturers at the conference. His preoccupation with Cleave's hypothesis made it inevitable that he should choose as his subject the relationship between diet and the diseases of Western culture.

Hugh Trowell who, back in 1956, had called Denis into his medical ward at Mulago Hospital to show him the lymphoma victim that had started him on the trail of the cause and cure of the disease, was in the audience.

Now, as Hugh listened to Denis's summary of Cleave's work and the list of diseases attributed by Cleave to the over-refining of carbohydrate foods, he recalled the book *Non-infective Diseases in Africa* which he had written in 1960, around the time he returned to England to train for the Anglican ministry. In this 450-page book he had referred to the diseases he had observed to be rare in Africa during the time he had worked there, from 1929.

The list was almost identical to that compiled by Cleave. In one chapter, on alimentary diseases, he had stated that all the non-infectious diseases of the large bowel common in Western countries were rare in Africans living south of the Sahara, where 'the natural diets are high in *fibre* content'. He suggested that much of this rarity could be ascribed to the protective action of fibre.

These references to the protection given by fibre in food were the result of a meeting which Hugh Trowell had had, back in 1947, with Alec Walker in Johannesburg. Trowell had been visiting South Africa to collect material for a book on the important nutritional disease of children, kwashiorkor.

During their discussions Walker had surprised Trowell by stating that he did not believe cereal fibre to be the harmful irritant of the digestive system that medical and nutritional opinion thought it to be. Because it was considered harmful, it was generally argued that fibre should be removed from cereal foods such as bread and rice.

The observations recorded by Trowell in his book attracted little attention. The book was not a success. Very few copies were sold when it was published in 1960. It was a great disappointment to Hugh Trowell, who had written the book during a period of great personal strain when his wife Peggy was becoming increasingly ill.

But now as, after the lecture, Hugh told Denis of his book and of the diseases it listed and of its reference to fibre, it was about to become an instrument of renewal. Its real value was to begin to be appreciated. From this point on there would be close collaboration between the two medical men, one a surgeon, the other a physician. They would work together in defining fibre and discovering more about its nature; in campaigning to promote fibre in diet as a protection against many Western diseases; and in dealing with initial opposition from the millers.

Back home in England, Hugh Trowell began to meet regularly with Denis. He would travel up from his Wiltshire home to spend time in the London office. The two men would discuss ideas for a book on diet and Western diseases. Denis was to be responsible for the chapters on the surgical aspects and Hugh to take charge of the medical side. Often they also spent time in prayer together.

Then Hugh would go to one of the medical libraries to find out all he could about fibre. The first essential was to be able to define it. Without a definition no serious study of the subject could be made and no book written. He expected this to be a simple task but, although he searched in libraries and medical bookshops, he could find no reference to fibre in food in any textbook of nutrition, medicine or surgery, or in any medical book. Only in books on botany was there any mention of plant fibre, and he found only one British food-table which referred to fibre, as a constituent of tropical food — but without defining it.

He set out to arrive at his own definition. Getting there was a long process which involved the expertise of other, younger nutrition experts. The first step was a decision to call the fibre they were interested in *dietary fibre*, the term now generally used. This distinguished it from the obsolete term *crude fibre* which relates only to that part of carbohydrate food which remains after boiling in dilute acid and then in dilute alkali.

(The acid/alkali test was originally designed in the first quarter of the nineteenth century for testing animal foods and had little relevance to the human consumption of fibre. It measured none of the now-recognized important components of fibre from the standpoint of human health.)

Hugh Trowell then went on to define dietary fibre. In layman's terms, it is the part of food which does not get digested in the small intestine but passes intact through it into the large intestine, where much of it is broken down by bacteria.

At the British Medical Association's medical library Hugh Trowell made a study of experiments which had been carried out to produce in animals the types of human diseases that could be regarded as typically Western. His particular interest was in those experiments where the animal had been fed diets containing cereal foodstuffs.

The reports did not contain detailed accounts of fibre content. But, for a meticulous researcher like Hugh Trowell, it was a simple matter to contact the animal foodstuff manufacturers and then put their figures into the results of the experiments. In this way he was able to show that feeding fibre-rich diets to the animals had actually prevented the formation of a number of the diseases which the experiments were aimed at inducing.

As the research continued Denis used every opportunity to promote in print and lectures the connection he saw between fibre-deficient diets and Western disease. He had begun tentatively, the year before his meeting with Hugh Trowell, with the publication in *The Lancet* of a short article with the title, 'Related Disease — Related Cause?' In it he argued that if several diseases occur in the same geographical locations, or in the same person, it could point to a common cause, as had been shown with Burkitt's lymphoma.

The following year, with the publication in *The Lancet* of an extended version of the original article, Denis was able to expand his theme to argue that what was true of lymphoma could also be true of Western diseases. If there were a common cause, it related to a deficiency of fibre in the diet. This was the start of 'fibre in the diet' becoming a catch-phrase. But not everyone was happy with the implied criticism of refined foods.

CHAPTER 16

Opposition

As early as June 1970 Denis found himself in public disagreement over his views on fibre with no less an authority than Professor Christiaan Barnard, the flamboyant South African heart-transplant surgeon. On 23 June the two men were taking part in a medical congress at Milner Park in Johannesburg. What they had to say was reported the next day in the South African newspaper, *The Daily News*.

Speaking on heart transplants, Professor Barnard said:

'I believe that we are born with an inability to handle certain fats and fatty acids. This genetic inability is the reason for heart disease.'

Denis did not agree:

'I don't think there is any evidence to support this hypothesis. I am convinced that heart disease is not due to hereditary factors at all but is related to Western civilization, mostly the food we eat.

'Indians in Natal have four times more heart disease than their cousins in Southern India. They have not altered genetically but their environment has changed.

'I am not in any sense criticizing Professor Barnard. He has studied the surgical treatment of heart disease and probably not the cause. I have done fairly extensive research on causes in recent years.'

Denis also came into conflict with other world experts over his conviction that lack of fibre could cause bowel cancer.

'One authority, who wrote a book on bowel cancer reflecting the medical opinion of the time, started off by saying in effect that the few people like Burkitt and Walker who believed fibre played a role in bowel cancer prevention could not be taken seriously. He spent the rest of his book talking about the role of fat in causing bowel cancer.

'Several years later I was invited to speak on fibre and bowel cancer at his Institute in New York. After that meeting my critic showed great guts by standing up when I had finished speaking and saying he could now see that both fibre and fat could be implicated in the occurrence of this tumour in different ways. The fact that fat appeared to be causative, he admitted, did not preclude the possibility that fibre might be protective.'

That converted expert went on to set up a team of researchers to work in Scandinavia, to follow up work which had previously been done by the International Agency for Cancer Research in Lyon, France. The aim was to discover why rural Finns had only one quarter the bowel cancer of the Copenhagen Danes. They had comparable life-styles and both ate the same amount of fat and protein. The only difference they could find was that the Finns ate twice as much fibre, mostly in the form of rye bread, and passed nearly twice as much stool.

It was an outcome which justified a golden rule Denis always applied when faced with opposition.

'When men oppose you, don't attack them. Keep on good terms with them and then when they switch round in their views they become good supporters.'

Not that everyone switched round in their views. As a result of Denis Burkitt's and Hugh Trowell's geographical and medical research they found themselves moving further away from Peter Cleave, who clung doggedly to his belief that sugar was the prime cause of Western diseases. Initially his reasoning that sugar was far more dangerous than flour, because it became eight times more concentrated when refined, had made good sense to Denis. But that was before the positive role of fibre in the bowel had been appreciated.

One particular piece of detective work, carried out by Hugh Trowell, was largely responsible for turning the spotlight on fibre rather than sugar. Cleave had always argued that sugar was the prime cause of diabetes. In this he had the support of Campbell, an acknowledged expert in diabetes, who had agreed with Cleave when he had attributed the rise and fall of diabetes mortalities between 1905 and 1947 to sugar consumption.

A graph in their book, *The Saccharine Disease*, seemed to provide positive proof of the connection between sugar in food and diabetes. It showed how diabetes declined during the food shortages of the First World War and again once sugar rationing was introduced during the Second World War.

But Trowell's quest for evidence had taken him to the British Nutrition Foundation, where he found figures to suggest that the introduction of the National Loaf during the war might be an alternative cause of the decline in diabetes. The National Loaf, made from less-refined flour, had been introduced to make the scarce supplies of wheat go further. It had been introduced at first voluntarily but later compulsorily, against the better judgement of some medical advisors, who were fearful for the digestive systems of the British people.

For Hugh Trowell the important fact was that the National Loaf contained 85 per cent whole wheat, compared with 72 per cent found in pre-war bread, and so it contained more fibre. Trowell's suspicions regarding the protection fibre was able to give against diabetes were further substantiated by the fact that a decline in diabetes continued after sugar rationing had ceased. It went on until bakeries stopped producing the high-fibre National Loaf.

Such findings made Hugh and Denis unpopular with Cleave, who found them unacceptable. There were periods when strained relations caused the two fibre men much distress.

To begin with, Hugh and Denis were not very popular with the British millers, either. Having been convinced for over 200 years that refined flour was best, and having geared up their production to meet the demands of a consuming public which also believed it, they did not take kindly to cranky medical men whose findings were appearing to prove them wrong.

It soon became clear to the two men that they were rocking the boat for many who had a vested interest in continuing to produce and promote refined flour. A couple of months after his confrontation with Christiaan Barnard, Denis approached the Director of the Nutrition Foundation in London to see if there was any possibility of publishing an article on fibre in the Foundation's *Bulletin*.

The director, Dorothy Hollingsworth, agreed to the idea and the manuscript which followed was immediately accepted for publication. But a few days later Denis received a phone call from the Foundation to say that the decision to publish had been reversed.

'I knew the BNF got some of its support from the millers, and I suspected that they did not want anyone saying that it was a bad thing taking fibre out of flour when they had spent the last 100 years developing better machinery for doing just that.'

A few days prior to the rejection, Denis had been lunching with Sir Ernst Chain, the physicist who was awarded the Nobel Prize for synthesizing penicillin. Sir Ernst had worked on fibre before becoming involved with penicillin. Over the meal he was interested to hear about Denis Burkitt's work.

Following the rejection the two men were in conversation again, this time over the telephone. Not realizing that the physicist had any inside knowledge of the BNF, Denis told him what had happened. He heard Sir Ernst chuckle. It turned out he was chairman of the Foundation's Scientific Advisory Committee. He promised to see about the controversial article, and it was published the following May in the BNF *Bulletin*, as originally planned.

There was general reluctance amongst editors of medical journals in the early 1970s to publish any article which attempted to link by a common cause those diseases which medical opinion generally regarded as quite separate. Denis was told categorically that no medical journal would be willing to accept any article linking a number of totally different diseases by a common cause.

A way round this barrier opened up when Denis was invited to give the Crookshank Memorial Lecture to the British Faculty of Radiologists at the Royal College of Surgeons, in May 1972. Without knowing that it would contain controversial material, the editor of the *British Medical Journal* asked beforehand if he could publish it.

Denis agreed, presuming that it would be subject to approval and would probably be rejected. To his surprise, although it contained arguments linking Western diseases, and in particular bowel cancer, with fibre deficiency in diets, his address was accepted for publication and published without any questions. The appearance of the article in such an important medical journal was a crucial breakthrough for Denis and for fibre in the diet. It attracted a lot of attention.

But even more attention was attracted by a television discussion that same year, as part of a BBC series *Down to Earth*. The programme was chaired by Kenneth Allsop and the subject was bread. A brief report of the programme published in the July 1972 issue of *Baking Industries Journal* showed that Denis was under attack but clearly able to defend himself. Nor was he the only member of the panel who came under attack from Allsop's penetrating questioning. With him on the panel, to represent the white flour side of the argument, was Dorothy Hollingsworth, director of BNF.

Allsop asked her if the white loaf was predominant simply because there was more profit to be made from it. The millers, he suggested, could sell the same loaf twice by extracting the bran first and selling that separately as cattle food.

Dorothy Hollingsworth did not agree: 'The public like white bread. They like purity and this has gone on for about 200 years.'

To the question of whether wholemeal bread was nutritionally better than white bread, she answered that there was something to be said on both sides.

Allsop then switched the questioning to Denis, to deal with the more serious aspect of the debate, concerning his contention made during the Crookshank Lecture that there were 'disturbingly strong links between white bread and the instances of many diseases, cancer included'.

Denis had to make it clear that he had been talking about cancer of the bowel in particular. Also he pointed out that it was not the white flour which concerned him but the removal of unabsorbed fibre, which had no nutrient value but was fundamental to the maintenance of health. He simply re-expressed his belief that the fundamental cause of many diseases in the West was the depletion of cereal fibre in the diet.

Transmission of the programme brought a swift response from the flour industry's spokesmen, the press office of the Flour Advisory Bureau. The following day it issued a lengthy press release. It was a detailed denial of the suggestions made in the programme and in the press that modern diet, and white bread in particular, was responsible for some Western diseases.

Here are some of the more critical paragraphs of the release, together with Denis Burkitt's own scribbled reactions to them (in brackets):

'The flour milling industry is much concerned that suggestions are being made, in papers in the medical press and elsewhere, that modern diet and particular items of diet such as white bread are responsible for an increase in diverticular disease and other diseases of the bowel . . .

'The basis of the theory which is now attempting to relate all these diseases to modern diet is that they are relatively common in those countries where the standard of living is high and rare amongst the peasants of Africa or Asia where the diet is not so sophisticated and the amount of roughage in the diet is very much higher.

'Taking this theory a step further, it is postulated that the diseases are more common in Western countries because of the much greater consumption of refined carbohydrates in the form of white bread and sugar which, it is claimed, results in a diet of low fibre or low residue contents. (certainly)

'The flour milling industry has been advised for many years, and continues to be advised, by the most eminent medical and scientific authorities available. Its advisors (who?) have reached the view that there is no convincing experimental or direct evidence to justify the existence of any link between diverticulosis and these other non-infective diseases of the bowel and diet in general, much less a link with individual items of our diet. (challenge)

'Much of the background evidence which has been advanced

is regarded as selective and many cogent factors appear to have been ignored. (such as?)

'In the context in question, comparison between the UK and primitive communities is not considered meaningful . . . Life expectancy is not comparable. Members of these primitive communities do not normally survive to the age level at which the middle-age complaints of our society occur. (not true)

'Against this background the industry affirms that in its view there is no evidence revealing any significant difference, in relation to health, between present-day white bread and wholemeal bread, both of which are extremely good and nutritious foods.

'Whether eaten as white or wholemeal, bread is our most important staple food and as Professor McCance, lately professor of experimental medicine at Cambridge, has pointed out: "Discussions on the relative merits of white and wholemeal bread are usually directed more by psychological bias than experimental fact."' (not true)

After two decades of experience in Africa, Denis Burkitt and Hugh Trowell were particularly upset by the assertion that people in primitive communities did not live to the age where they would get middle-age complaints. They knew that this just was not true.

'Admittedly relatively few Africans reached middle age but that was because of the high infant mortality rates. Alec Walker had already shown that in South Africa, around Johannesburg, the black people that did reach middle age had a better chance of reaching old age than the white people of the same region.'

The two men also found galling the suggestion in the Bureau's press release that adequate facilities for diagnosis of diseases were lacking in Africa. After working in teaching hospitals in Africa both believed that autopsies were carried out with the same care as in England.

Because of the statements in the Bureau's release which Denis considered misleading, or just not true, he asked the press office if it would name the scientific advisors it had referred to, and say what evidence it had for its claims.

The Bureau refused. But it did offer Denis and Hugh a

chance to meet some of the senior representatives of the British millers. At the meetings it was clear that the views of the two medical men were diametrically opposed to those of the millers, whose machines were busy churning out refined white flour and bread. So no agreements were reached. But the atmosphere was friendly and it led to Denis being asked to present his side of the story at the next AGM of the Millers' Association.

In thanking Denis, after he had presented his case at the AGM, the chairman remarked that beforehand he had had visions of press headlines referring to 'Daniel in the lions' den' or 'David meets Goliath'. But having heard him speak he felt sure it was more likely to be, 'The lamb lies down with the wolves'.

Some time later Denis commented:

'Direct attacks on those in the milling industry as if they were deliberate rogues are never justified or fruitful. Many well-meaning dietary enthusiasts have regrettably adopted this aggressive attitude. But my approach has been that an increased demand by the consumer for brown or wholemeal bread will inevitably be met by increased productivity in the industry.'

And so it has proved to be, to the benefit of both the millers and the consuming public.

Discussion with the millers went on for about a year. They were terminated when it was agreed that the chairman should ask the government for its committee on medical aspects of nutrition, the COMA committee, to investigate the matter.

Denis did not expect the committee to come up with a quick answer. Its acronym, COMA, was he said appropriate. But he did not expect it to take nearly a decade before it published its findings. In fact the committee was not convened until after the Royal College of Physicians had set up its own committee to consider and report on the medical aspects of dietary fibre.

COMA's findings were published nine years later. They contained recommendations that the consumption of brown and wholemeal bread should be increased and that more of this bread should be provided in public eating-places. They were findings which gave Denis and Hugh a great deal of satisfaction, after waiting and campaigning for so long.

In the United States, where Denis always received a more positive reaction to his views, the government acted rather more speedily. By 1977 the US Senate Committee on Nutrition and Human Needs had collected evidence from a great number of nutrition experts, including Trowell and Cleave, so that it could advise the American public on what was a healthy diet. (Denis had been invited to testify, but on the same day had been asked to present his case before the American Food and Drugs Administration (FDA).) It recommended an increased consumption of starch and dietary fibre, and a reduced intake of fat, sugar and salt. Its basic recommendations have since been embodied in national reports from many Western countries, including Great Britain.

CHAPTER 17

Travel

From the time Denis returned home to England with his family from Uganda in 1966 he travelled extensively throughout the world. He frequently spent over two months a year abroad and away from Olive. It began with his twice-yearly safaris through East, West and South Africa, making contact with doctors in mission and government hospitals. These were followed by similar visits to Asia and the Middle East. His aim was to initiate or encourage the continued co-operation of doctors in supplying information about disease distribution.

Increasingly he found his trips to the third world interspersed with invitations to tell the people of North America about his findings. There was still an interest in his lymphoma work. But as he became more outspoken about the effects of diet on Western diseases, bowel cancer in particular, so this began to dominate his lectures, informal talks and press and radio interviews.

From the early 1970s he was making an average of four trips a year across the Atlantic. Mostly he would be invited by a medical establishment, college or university to speak at a conference, or deliver a memorial address. Those who invited him paid his transatlantic air fare. Then other individuals or organizations would hear of the proposed visit and ask him to speak at their institutions in exchange for accommodation, local travel, expenses and perhaps a fee.

From all these invitations would emerge a tightly-run schedule with two or even three engagements a day for up to two weeks, in which he crossed and recrossed the American continent in order to include as many centres as possible.

Between these commitments he would also fit in visits that suited his own interests. It was during such trips, for example, that he found time to visit the Eskimos in Alaska, the Pima Indians of Arizona and Mexico, and the religious communities of California and Utah.

And from contacts he made at conferences and meetings he was also able to learn about disease patterns in places he had not been able to visit. It was on a trip to Hawaii that he learned from Ian Prior, head of epidemiology at Wellington University Medical School in New Zealand, the fate of emigrating Polynesian people whose health had suffered once they reached New Zealand and took up Western life-styles. It was a similar story with the Maori people moving into the cities.

Although Denis learned a great deal on his American tours, his main object was to impart rather than gather information.

During his early tours, the American medical profession were just as sceptical of his fibre theories as their colleagues in Britain. The press may have caught a vision of what he was saying at the 1971 Cancer Congress in San Diego, where he had been invited to give his first paper on bowel cancer and diet. But only a small minority of cancer research workers were prepared to take his fibre hypothesis seriously.

Eight years later, opinions had decidedly changed. Denis was at an international conference on colo-rectal (bowel) cancer, open only to invited delegates and held in New York. In a summary of that conference it was agreed that, whatever might be responsible for causing this form of cancer, dietary fibre almost certainly played a protective role.

Denis must accept much of the credit for the change of view which had taken place in the intervening years. It was that Burkitt singlemindedness which had already brought about the discovery of Burkitt's lymphoma and its cure. His enthusiasm, persistence, and sheer ability to communicate with conviction the truth as he saw it, eventually bore fruit. And he was willing to go anywhere to proclaim that truth.

Travel was never wasted time. There were books to read (he

enjoyed the biographies of Christian men and women); people to talk to; and letters to write home. His letters to Olive and the girls, written at airports, or high above the Atlantic, or while flying over some new country scene, or from some too-luxurious hotel, expose the personal side of Denis Burkitt's very public life. They reveal his interest in the details of other people and of other places. They also reveal his own values.

The letters written to Olive on his visit to North America in February 1975, are typical. It was an averagely-busy year in which he also managed to make extensive tours of East Africa and the Far East.

Somewhere over the Atlantic on his way to Montreal, Denis began his first letter home:

'My Darling,
'Soon you will be getting yourself a simple supper. We got off at 1.45 p.m. Served lunch at 3. Time must be allowed for the indispensable drinks. There is a South African sitting next to me. He actually recognized me from photos he'd seen and had read a lot of my work. How remarkable. He works for a large chemical company. I have read the first fifty pages of *The Hiding Place*.

'Thursday, 6.45 a.m. Martin Lewis met me at the airport. All is white in snow. Drive to absurdly luxurious hotel. Even the towel I used on arrival had been replaced by bedtime. I got to the hotel about 5 p.m. Had a bath and was collected at 6 for a 6.30 meeting. All interiors are so hot that people wear thin summer suits as in Uganda. (The temperature outside was well below freezing.) I need not have brought my heavy suit . . .

'I was back in my hotel by 8 p.m. and went to bed. Took Mogadon and slept for nine hours. Colour TV in my room. Continental breakfast £1! I think of John Taylor's book, *Enough is Enough* . . . As always a magnificent Gideon Bible in my room. In English and French. It looks so unused, but this may not be so.

'Montreal is a bigger city than Toronto. I hadn't expected that. Grey-dull light snow — 8.45 a.m. Had a good breakfast.

Could discard my warm vest. This living in an artificial hot-house must almost preclude outside activities.

'7 Feb. Over Canada.

'I lectured this morning 10 to 11. Then driven to airport. Flew 12.45. Now flying over flat white Canada, marked with black lines of roads and partly obscured by clouds. I feel that my time in Montreal was very rewarding and usefully used.'

Denis had spent two days in Montreal. He had visited the McGill Medical School and given several lectures on diet and Western diseases, both at the department of surgery and at pathology institutes. He was now flying Canadian Pacific to Edmonton, Alberta. There, in sub-zero temperatures, he was met by his old friend and companion of the long safari, Cliff Nelson, who was now working at the Allin Clinic in Edmonton.

'Saturday 8th.

'This morning was so very interesting, enjoyable and profitable in one of the large hospitals (Royal Alexandra Hospital). I got just the information I needed on several things. All the Nelsons are home — Beth, the two boys and two girls. Snow is so lovely in the sun. I had a call last night from Wisconsin. They would like me to spend two days there at two different universities in April.'

Denis goes on to tell Olive how Cliff and Beth took him on a tour of Edmonton before attending a Christian Medical Fellowship dinner at which he gave the address. Sunday morning was spent at the Nelsons' church. Denis spoke to Cliff's adult Bible class.

'Very good morning service. 700 people present. $4,000 taken up.'

In the evening he preached at Beulah Alliance Church. Monday and Tuesday were full days.

'Monday 10 Feb. This morning we left at 7.40 for the Royal Alexandra Hospital. I spoke to a packed auditorium at 8.30 and was well received. Then to the University Hospital sixteen miles away for informal discussions with surgeons, followed by lunch and then lectures 1 to 2. Spent 2.30 to 4 with residents and then sixteen miles in the snow back to Royal Alexandra for dinner.

'Tuesday. At 8.30 a.m. I spoke on the phone to a radio interviewer and it went simultaneously on the air. Then to a hospital where Eskimos are treated, so that I could talk to members of the staff. Then to the Cross Cancer Hospital to lecture on bowel cancer and have lunch — and thence to the airport where I am now writing.

'The temperature today is about 26° below zero but it is bright and sunny and the air is so dry and still that it doesn't feel all that cold.'

Next stop was Saskatoon in Saskatchewan, where he wrote home:

'Seems so long since we parted. I came across a great verse in Jude encompassing us both. "Live in the love of God and in the safe-keeping of Jesus Christ".'

He went on: 'Keep warm and put up the heating as required. I would love to have you with me but you could do little except read and do your tapestry. It's too cold to go out.'

For Denis the cold did not last long. Four days later, having lectured at the University of Saskatchewan, he was on a Jumbo jet over the Pacific, heading for the much warmer climate of Hawaii. In Honolulu he was to attend the thirteenth Pan-Pacific Surgical Association Congress.

'I have finished Corrie ten Boom's *The Hiding Place*. What a rebuke when one ever complains about circumstances. The enormous relief and healing power of Christ-enabled forgiveness! . . .'

From his hotel room in Honolulu he wrote again to Olive:

'Sunday Feb. 16 — 4.30 a.m. I sit up in bed in a situation of luxury almost unparalleled in my experience. My room is on the twenty-eighth floor of the Hilton Hawaiian Village Hotel.

Large full-length sliding-glass windows on two sides open up on to small balconies with a sea of lights beyond. What will appear at daylight I don't yet know.

'We landed at Honolulu 5 p.m. local time. Had I come on the flight the agents had booked me on I would, like the other conference delegates, have been garlanded with a wreath of flowers. This apparently is one of the premier American surgical conferences and I wouldn't be surprised if there were well over 2,000 surgeons, with their wives. They wander about in their light summer attire.

'Even in the few hours I have been here the stark materialism overwhelms me. "Come and enjoy yourselves and pay lots for it" is the cry. And all this after reading Corrie ten Boom's book.

'But of course I intend to make the very best use of my few days here. Only lamenting my aloneness. Ralph and Ruth (Blocksma) arrive today. I will have my quiet time now and watch the dawn appear through my open window.'

The next day, Monday, was the first day of the conference.

'I was up at 6 and was the first speaker at a 7.30 a.m. meeting. This was an opportunity. Surgeons from about sixty countries. Reading books and articles in no way compares with the great privilege of being able to discuss problems with people — and, to alert them to start looking, I spoke on preventing diseases — the other three speakers spoke only on techniques for curing them. In the hour's discussion afterwards there was only one question on prevention. This is typical of the surgical approach.'

This theme of prevention versus cure was going to play an increasingly important part in Denis's thinking in the years ahead.

'How I wish you could sit here with me and look at the sun-bathed sea and beaches and the mass concentration of boats. I am very conscious that you bear the brunt and cost of my being here — and in all I gain the credit must go, as in the case of

David's men, to the one who "stays by the stuff".

'In twenty minutes I go to the hospital where the great studies relating disease patterns between Japanese in Japan and Japanese in Hawaii are done. Studies I have so often quoted but will now have the opportunity of seeing in reality.'

Later that day, at 8.30 p.m., he added to his letter:

'I believe I have really been able to stimulate an American professor of surgery into doing a trial of intestinal behaviour, contrasting American blacks and whites. This should be really worth while. I spoke to him this morning and he rang me this evening for details. Could you ask Sandra (Denis's assistant in London) to post to him by air about 1,000 plastic pellets, plus instructions.

'Ralph and Ruth and I had dinner together. I signed for all three as I have hardly used my free-meal service, being asked out so much. In fact I have been offered a week's hotel expenses but am only using four days. Of course Ralph and Ruth were so lovingly asking after you. Ralph is also an invited speaker, like me. All speakers are selected and invited, which keeps the standard high . . .

'Tuesday, 6.30 a.m. I will post this today and try to ring you from Halifax (Nova Scotia). A week tomorrow I'll be starting for home.'

He began his next letter to Olive the following day, just after taking off from Honolulu.

'2.30 p.m. From the air I got a good view of my hotel. I feel that I am racing towards you at 600 m.p.h. On the outward journey I was approaching you in time but not in space. Now I am approaching you in both ways.

'My time here was so rewarding. When talking to Ian Prior (the man who had told him about the Polynesian people) the thought germinated of trying to link together in some form of informal association people like Ian, Alec Walker and myself, who are working in our field of epidemiology. Ian, who has just turned down the offer of a university chair in favour of continuing his work in epidemiology, jumped at this suggestion.

'The geographical sessions this morning went well. Ian and I were amongst the speakers. Many surgeons came up to talk afterwards and I was able to show them what bran was. Ian said at the end of his presentation that if I was ever to be elevated to the peerage — God forbid — I should be "Lord Burkitt of Bran".

'Ian also referred to the "Burkitt hypothesis", so I told the audience it should be Cleave's hypothesis, which I had merely expanded and modified.

'There is no doubt whatever that it is the few personal contacts made that in the long run count most.

'The plane is very empty. I have never yet felt really tempted to pay $2.50 to look at the in-flight film. I am enjoying the Agatha Christie I borrowed. It is eight hours since breakfast, so I look forward to lunch. I could hardly call epidemiological research a tough life, other than the horrible separation. Your second letter arrived safely. Thank you so much for it. The captain has just told us we are seven miles above the sea.'

In Halifax, Nova Scotia, Denis kept his promise to phone Olive. He spent the following three days at Dalhousie University, giving lectures on cancer of the colon, holding informal meetings with the students and staff, and being interviewed by CBC television and the local press. He also made ward rounds of the Nova Scotia tumour clinic and spoke at another Christian Medical Fellowship; then it was home to meet Olive, who was waiting for him at Heathrow airport.

During all his lecture tours overseas Denis took advantage of every opportunity to speak at Christian meetings, particularly those organized by the Christian Medical societies. He was also ready, at secular meetings, to testify to the importance of his Christian faith in his medical work. His American tour at the beginning of 1975 was no exception.

But few occasions had such an influence on him as his visit to Singapore in November 1975, when he was one of the UK delegates to the fifth International Congress of Christian

Physicians. Denis wrote home in long and glowing terms of his experience there.

'Singapore 6/11/75. We arrived here Monday evening after an eighteen-hour flight, stopping at Zürich, Bahrain and Colombo.

'The organization, done by Christian Chinese doctors, is superb. There are some 600 doctors and wives and 150-200 students. The opening ceremony last night was a model of attention to detail. Probably 800 there. The 150-strong US contingent came straight from the airport and arrived just in time. The president of the Republic is a Christian and gave a good opening speech . . .

'There was an opening session with university students, boys and girls plus a band, singing beautifully and all so neat and orderly. A Chinese girl sang "The Lord is my Shepherd" as a solo and Stanley Browne delivered a magnificent and scholarly address. The whole spirit of the gathering was a marvellous start to a conference of this nature . . .

'I met many of my American friends in the hotel afterwards, including Ray Knighton and his son Tom, straight from Bangladesh. They just got out before the coup . . .

'Today the first devotional Bible study was to a packed auditorium in the hotel followed by an excellent talk on ethical problems given by Ronald Winton, chairman of the WHO committee on ethics in medicine. I missed the second half of the morning. After coffee I went with two Indian surgeons to meet surgeons at the Singapore General Hospital.

'This afternoon there were four excellent short talks and discussion. On ethical problems including abortion and counselling the dying . . . of course the most valuable part is the personal contacts . . .

'Friday. Last night I spoke on "My faith and my work" to a full lecture theatre of medical students. There is a very strong Christian Union here and some 20 per cent of the university doctors are Christians, as are the wardens of all the student halls of residence. And I mean really committed Christians. I spoke on the ill-effects of food deficiencies, including fibre, for biological man and went on to the ill-effects of leaving God out of our lives.'

'Sunday. This morning's cathedral service was the highlight of the whole week. It brought tears to my eyes to stand in that great throng of so many nations worshipping God. The bishop (a Chinese) is a real man of God. I think it was the most impressive service I have ever attended.

'The communion service was incorporated and at one stage we all shook hands with our neighbours. There was great orderliness, dignity and reverence with freedom, love and friendship. How I would have loved to have you with me. I consider this the best organized conference I have ever attended.'

If Denis was impressed by the Congress, there were others attending who were just as impressed with him. One Christian first-year medical student, Low Cheng Ooi, reporting on the event in the magazine *Vagus*, ends his report full of praise for him.

'In my mind,' wrote Low Cheng Ooi, 'of all the great personalities that attended the conference one person clearly stood out among the rest. He is none other than Dr Denis Burkitt of Burkitt's lymphoma fame. In him I saw a man of great wisdom and knowledge, yet also a man who is humble and knows that his all is from God. The testimony of his work and his faith was one which I found truly inspiring.'

CHAPTER 18

Media Response

Apart from occasional references to 'appreciative audiences', the detailed accounts which Denis sent to Olive during his trips to North America and elsewhere conveyed no impression of the impact he was having on other people, in particular the impact of his fibre-in-the-diet message. But the impact was there.

It may have taken the medical profession a decade to acknowledge the validity of what he was saying, but he quickly caught the imagination of the media, as newspaper reports during and immediately after his 1975 visit to Halifax, Nova Scotia, show. They were quite typical of many published in the mid-1970s.

The day after Denis had spoken at Dalhousie University under the headline 'Doctor says removal of cereal fibre was a dietary disaster', the medical reporter of the *Halifax Mail-Star* wrote:

'Denis Burkitt, the British surgeon who ushered in the modern era of chemotherapy in treatment of cancer,* linked white bread and constipation with cancer of the colon when he spoke in Halifax yesterday. The eminent doctor was giving the second annual Margaret and Norman Gosse Memorial Lecture, and his audience filled the lecture hall seats and aisles. Overflow audiences watched on television screens in a nearby hall.

'Speaking with a disarming, single-syllable candour, he said many scientists go to other countries and determine the level

*Denis Burkitt himself does not acknowledge the truth of this claim.

of research taking place by the numbers of microscopes and computers in use. "When I go to a country, I ask, 'What is the size of the stool you pass every day?' I've been in North America for two weeks and haven't seen a decent stool yet".'

The reporter goes on to describe Denis's morning walks in Uganda and Nepal, to photograph stools by the roadside.

'"You do this," he said, "and people think you are totally mad . . . You have to accept this".'

But the 1975 visit to North America was not the first to fire the media's imagination over fibre. It had really begun following the 1971 San Diego conference on cancer of the colon and rectum, at which Denis had given his invited paper linking the cancer to diet. That was the beginning of a mounting interest, which reached its first peak with the publication in December 1974 of an article in the American edition of *The Readers Digest*.

The article by Lawrence Galton, whose book *The truth about fibre in your diet* was published two years later, was remarkable not so much for what it said as for the impact which *The Readers Digest* claimed it had on the magazine's readers. A year after the article appeared, the publishers ran an advert in the consumer trade press, under the heading, 'How a doctor's study of primitive people doubled an American industry'.

The advert plotted a chart, claiming August 1974 as the time the American public started to hear about Denis Burkitt's fibre findings. By November, the sales of fibre-rich products were up 16 per cent. Then came *The Readers Digest* article in December. By the next February, sales were up 58 per cent and by September a total of 104 per cent. The advert argued very convincingly that much of the growth was due to the fact that *The Readers Digest* went into 18 million American homes.

An editorial in *Advertising Age* backed up *The Readers Digest* claims. It talks of the fibre theory as 'hitting the American market-place' as a result of the article, which clearly outlines the research leading up to the theory, giving equal space to all those who had some hand in its formulation.

The *Advertising Age* editorial also carried a quote from the director of public affairs at Kellogg's, Dr Gary Costley, who says the article 'started an avalanche here'.

In fairness it has to be said that a number of other popular American magazines also published articles on fibre and on Denis Burkitt's work during the period from August 1974 to September 1975 — *Time Magazine, Ladies Circle* and *Saturday Evening Post* among them. Also the major manufacturers of breakfast cereal — Kellogg's, General Foods and Nabisco — were all running advertising campaigns which began to focus attention on a 'back-to-nature' style.

The significance of *The Readers Digest* article for the fibre story was its indication that an advertising agency of the status of J. Walter Thompson, who handled *The Readers Digest* account, should have seen Denis Burkitt's message as a powerful tool for the promotion of its own client's product.

Wherever he travelled abroad Denis could expect the media to be waiting for him: the newspapers, radio microphones and television cameras. This was particularly so on his 1975 visit to Australia. He flew to Perth on 17 April and returned on 4 May. Hardly one of those eighteen busy days of lectures and meetings went by without the press, radio or TV stations making some demand on his time — in Perth, Sydney, Hobart in Tasmania, and Melbourne.

When he arrived in Perth from London via Bombay, Denis was the first to leave the plane. In a letter to Olive he explains why:

'It is 6 p.m. Monday — 5 a.m. with you. The health official who came aboard at Perth asked for a *Professor* Burkitt and then brought me off the plane, even before the first-class passengers. (He did not believe in travelling first class, even when his trip was paid for.) It didn't help much as I still had to wait for my luggage . . . The TV and press people were waiting for me.'

The following Friday he wrote from Sydney:

'I was met at Sydney airport by Dr Jim Isbister and driven to his home. Yesterday morning I was driven to a radio station for an interview. Then to a university hospital where I met Bob Claxton, a Christian who was a member of Makerere and Mulago staff after we left. The professor of surgery here had

been on the same army draft as I was from Mombasa to
Colombo in 1944.

'After a sandwich lunch I lectured to an appreciative
audience. Then was driven to a very modern Seventh-Day
Adventist hospital about ten miles away. Like a Hilton Hotel. I
had both TV and press interviews and later was guest of honour
at a beautiful dinner. About thirty selected guests, mainly
medical families, including the dean of the university. Non-
alcoholic grape and apple drinks, beautifully served. A de-
lightful vegetarian supper with grace said beforehand.

'I was asked to say a few words afterwards and then we all
went to an almost new lecture hall with a gallery . . . I spoke
for nearly an hour and then was flooded with questions. They
were all so kind and welcoming. My hosts got me home just
before 11.

'This morning I was collected 8.30 and driven some fifty
miles south to Wollongong, a far bigger place than I ever
imagined. There I had a TV interview followed by a lecture at
the university to nurses, doctors and non-medicals — then a
press interview. No time for lunch so my host, a worker for the
College of General Practitioners, got some bananas and sand-
wiches to eat in the car.'

For Denis it had been just another couple of busy days. But
perhaps the busiest day of his Australian tour was still to come.
On the following Thursday, in Melbourne, he wrote in his
diary:

'Very full day. Blood test taken. Spoke briefly to Worburton
staff. Then with Harley to Melbourne. Gave *seven* interviews
with TV, radio, press and video tape between 10.15 and 5.15 at
Family Doctor Centre. Then dinner at College of General
Practitioners. Then open lecture.'

The British media also caught something of the vision of
Denis Burkitt's work. There was less excitement than in
America and Australia, partly no doubt because a 'prophet is
not without honour except in his own country' but also because
in the 1970s Britain was behind these other countries in its
health consciousness. Nevertheless articles making reference to
the fibre theory and crediting Denis as its chief protagonist did

appear in the main daily and weekend papers and their colour supplements.

One minor British boost to the work of Denis Burkitt and Hugh Trowell was the publication in 1975 of the book they had been preparing ever since their reunion in 1970. *Refined Carbohydrate Foods and Disease: some implications of dietary fibre*, published by Academic Press, was a medical book for the academics and not designed to attract popular reviews. Nevertheless it did attract attention and gave some publicity to fibre, since it contained most of the geographical and medical evidence which the two men had accumulated over the previous five years.

Two publications which carried lengthy reviews were *Doctor* and *The Irish Press*. Both quoted at length from the foreword written by Sir Richard Doll who described the book as an exciting medical adventure:

'Once in every ten years or so,' wrote Doll, 'a new idea emerges about the cause of diseases that captures the imagination and, for a time, seems to provide a key to the understanding of many of those diseases of which the etiology (cause) was previously unknown.

'To these we may now add a deficiency of dietary fibre. Whether it will be as seminal an idea as vitamin deficiency, or as sterile as that of stress, we shall probably not know for another ten years.'

The book was largely the work of Denis Burkitt and Hugh Trowell. But it had other contributors, among them Dr Ken Heaton, whom Denis had met during a visit to Bristol University to lecture on diet and disease at the invitation of Tony Epstein. After that particular lecture, Ken Heaton, who had been in the audience, told Denis that he too had been influenced by Cleave's hypothesis on sugar. From that point on, Heaton, who was a senior consultant lecturer in medicine at the university, became closely identified with the work the two men were doing on fibre research.

Some of the secular publications which described Denis's work made reference to his strong Christian faith. There were those for whom it formed an irresistible link, an opportunity to create a catchy headline that referred in a variety of ways to the 'missionary intent on spreading the fibre gospel with evangelical zeal'. Other journalists, interested in seeing the whole man, had obviously been struck by Denis's sincerity during the natural course of an interview.

'He is deeply religious', reported *The Observer*. 'Burkitt's life is shaped by Christian faith', echoed *The Sunday Times*.

Understandably it was the Christian press which made the most of this now famous man's spiritual recipe for living. Towards the end of 1975, the year before Denis was due to retire from the Medical Research Council at sixty-five, Roger Day of *Crusade* (now *Today*) magazine visited Denis in his Tottenham Court Road office to hear about his faith and his work.

'I met Denis Burkitt in his unpretentious office in Tottenham Court Road. For one so eminent in cancer research he is remarkably ordinary, with no delusions of grandeur. His secretary walks in and out of his office at will. The visitor's chair is beside his own, behind an antiquated desk. His office is far from neat but is obviously a hive of activity. And his far from superior brief-case, plastered with torn airline labels, has seen better days.'

As Roger Day later reports, the interview clearly revealed Denis Burkitt's priorities for life:

'If I was asked what has been the greatest blessing in my life as a Christian I would say my family, because being "successful" is absolutely unimportant compared to happiness at home.'

And what, asked Day, was the most important aspect of his Christian life?

'A deliberate time daily for Bible study and prayer. I get up in the morning and make my wife a cup of tea. We have a good long morning kiss. Then we have our half-hour quiet time.

'I hope it will be some encouragement to people to realize that I was never a bright kind of guy. I was an absolute mug at everything at school and I never really began to get prizes for anything until I went to university. I don't think I have a high IQ but I've had wonderful opportunities and wonderful colleagues.

'As my friend Alf Stanway (then Bishop of Central Tanganyika) said to me: "Anything you give to God in teaspoonsful he gives back to you in shovelsful." I thought I was giving up surgery going to Africa and yet I had a vastly more rewarding surgical and research career than I'd ever have had if I'd stayed at home. And now when I come into the office and open up my post I'm like a boy opening his Christmas stocking.'

Knowing that Denis Burkitt was due to retire from the Medical Research Council the following year, Roger Day asked him if he planned to retire from his research. He replied that he had already accepted an honorary appointment at St Thomas's Hospital. It would at least give him an office in London from which to carry on his work.

'I feel my work will be going on. I've got engagements up to the end of 1977 at various places, I enjoy my work so much and openings are increasing rather than diminishing in the way of opportunities and invitations.'

And so it proved. Very little changed when Denis finally moved out of his 'unpretentious office' in Tottenham Court Road and took up his new appointment as Honorary Senior Research Fellow at St Thomas's Hospital. Here an equally unpretentious office gave him a professionally respectable address in London from which to continue his epidemiological research. He also had secretarial assistance with his papers and tour correspondence.

The only big change resulting from his retirement was a drop in income. Having always been abstemious, never spending money unnecessarily, this did not present too much of a problem. There were still fees from his lecture tours and royalties from his books and he had been promised some support from industry for his modest research expenses.

The request for industrial support had followed on from the Medical Research Council's inability to continue their support for his research work after retirement. He had worked hard putting his case to the MRC and the rejection was a disappointment. But it was one from which he soon recovered, seeing it simply as a positive lead to a new avenue.

Recording his thoughts on the matter while attending a Kellogg's symposium in Nova Scotia he began that day's diary entry with a scripture quotation — 'He brought us out . . . that he might bring us in' — and went on to write: 'When God closes one door he opens another. The MRC turning down my grant application is being followed by a better door opening.'

Over many years of lecturing, Denis had accumulated a large number of slides, cartoons and diagrams. After his retirement, he began thinking about ways of using some of these as the basis for a popular illustrated book on the role of fibre in human nutrition. He wrote a couple of sample chapters and sent them, together with the illustrations, to several medical publishers. His work was repeatedly rejected. He put the material away in a drawer in his office and accepted the defeat.

Then, in 1977, a young editor came to see him. Martin Dunitz had just set up his own publishing house and had heard of Denis Burkitt's work through a friend. Would he consider writing an illustrated book on some aspect of diet for the popular reader? Denis remembers that day vividly.

'I opened the drawer and showed him the manuscript that had been so often rejected. I told him that the only aspect of diet I could write about was fibre. He accepted the idea and so I started on my first book aimed at the man in the street.'

The book needed no research. All the material was already available in the much larger work he and Hugh Trowell had published two years earlier. There were also many filed and indexed articles and papers to hand.

The title of the book, first published in October 1979 in Britain, Canada and Australia was, *Don't forget fibre in your diet*. Subsequently it was also published in America with the title, *How to eat right to keep fit and enjoy life more*. Denis did not like that title and in later editions the English title was adopted in America.

In under five years the book was translated into nine other languages and by the time the fourth edition appeared in 1983 some 200,000 copies had been sold. Most importantly for Denis, this popular book brought his fibre-in-the-diet recipe for health to the ordinary person in a way that had not been done before.

CHAPTER 19

The Man and his Message

Writing in the *British Medical Journal* in July 1983, Michael O'Donnell recounted how, a few years earlier, he had spoken at a medical society in Durham where Denis Burkitt had been the guest speaker at the previous meeting. O'Donnell's host told him that by 11 a.m. the following day Durham had sold out of bran, so persuasive had Denis's lecture been.

After hearing that, O'Donnell always made a point, when speaking at any medical gathering, to ask if Denis Burkitt had been there before him.

'I would discover that his visit had two invariable effects: a record turn-out of members, followed by a local sell-out of bran.'

Eventually Dr O'Donnell caught up with Denis and was able to judge for himself his lecturing capabilities and persuasive powers.

'I was not disappointed,' wrote O'Donnell in the *BMJ*. 'His lectures really are remarkable. He uses no rhetorical devices as, with compelling power, he adduces the evidence that suggests lack of fibre in our diet begets many of our Western ailments.

'He grabs the audience's attention not with gimmicks but with inexorable arguments. And never once does he sound a crank, not even when he is exhorting his listeners to examine their stools to see whether they float or sink — a simple guide to whether they contain enough fibre.'

Denis Burkitt's success as a communicator, whether lecturing on geographical pathology, his Christian faith, or fibre in the diet, stems from a total belief based on personal experience that what he is saying is true. But there is also that added quality which compels even those who disagree with him to pay attention, a charismatic ability to communicate original ideas in a compelling, yet basic and often witty way.

One reporter summed him up as 'a fast talker, full of wit and irreverence for conventional thinking'.

Any attempt to reduce one of the lectures to print inevitably loses much of that fast wit, along with the soft Irish lilt of his voice. But the full impact of his message still remains, as the following transcript shows. It is a shortened and edited version (he usually speaks for forty-five minutes non-stop) of a lecture he gave in June 1984 to a medical audience in Doncaster.

'It has been said that as doctors we tend to look too much on patients as machines. When the machine goes wrong we bring into play all our expertise and technology and equipment to identify and, if possible, repair the fault. We give little thought to the environment in which the machine runs.

'The gist of my talk to you tonight is that we ought to be more concerned with the environment in which the patient lives.

'A document published in the United States last June by the National Research Council contained the statement that people in the US will eventually have the option to reduce the incidence of total cancer by at least one-third by stopping smoking and that another third could be prevented through changes in diet.

'The authors of the document are saying that we can reduce our total cancer risk by no less than two-thirds by altering our life-style. And tonight I am going to argue that this applies even more so to those other diseases that are filling surgeries and hospital beds in England today.

'But first let us look for a moment at how we conquered infective diseases as a major cause of death in this country. Until fifty years ago these were the commonest causes of death throughout the world. They still are in third-world countries, but no longer so in the West.

'Mortality rates from many infectious diseases fell dramatically between the middle of the last century and the Second

World War, and this occurred *before any effective treatment had become available*. So we must be honest with ourselves as doctors and admit that it was not therapy that conquered infective diseases, but the provision of clean water, adequate sewage disposal, improved nutrition and in some areas immunization.

'I used to labour under the delusion that doctors and medicine had a profound effect on the health of a community. This I now see as a total fallacy. They have a profound effect on sick people and sick people are very important. But you never reduce the frequency of a disease by improving its treatment. I've had to ask myself several times over the past year: Has any disease been reduced significantly because of improved treatment? With the possible exception of some highly contagious diseases, the answer is, "No".

'I spent twenty very happy years as a surgeon in Africa. I enjoyed it all. I helped some people, I hope. I helped to train some African surgeons. But let me be honest. I made no impact whatsoever on the health of the community I served. If I had spent my twenty years in charge of a team digging wells and latrines I would have done far more for the health of the community.

'I'm not sorry I did what I did, but the point I want to make is that it is of little use doing curative medicine unless we are also doing something to prevent disease.

'Immunization has of course been enormously successful — in this country against diseases such as diphtheria and polio-myelitis, and in the third world against yellow fever. And perhaps the greatest medical advance of the century has been the abolition of smallpox throughout the world: in this case elimination was achieved not by improving the treatment but by eradicating the cause. We have to identify causes before we can eradicate them.

'As infective diseases have fallen as major causes of death in this country they have been replaced by a new set of diseases, the non-infective diseases which are increasingly referred to as *Western Diseases* because they are characteristic of modern Western culture. Here are some of them.

'Appendicitis is predominantly a disease of modern Western culture. For nearly three years we circulated 150 up-country African hospitals every month, asking for reports on any patients suffering from appendicitis. We found about one patient per hospital per year. Thirty years ago I wrote a paper on abdominal surgery in Africa. At that time, in a 600-bed teaching hospital in Uganda, we admitted two patients a year with appendicitis. And without exception they came from the upper strata of society there. A hospital of this size in Britain might admit two patients a day.

'My professor of surgery in Africa, Sir Ian McAdam, would teach his young surgeons in training never to diagnose appendicitis in an African unless the patient could speak English! Nobody in East Africa gets appendicitis until they have learned to speak English. It is an index of contact with Western culture.

'Diverticular disease is a disease of Western culture, almost unknown in the third world. Even in a relatively advanced city like New Delhi, where I visited an enormous university X-ray department, I found they had seen only eight cases of diverticular disease in thirteen years. In Britain it is estimated that it is present in one in three adults over sixty.

'Cancer of the large bowel is more closely related to Western culture than is any other form of cancer. After lung tumours, colo-rectal cancer is the second commonest cause of cancer death in economically more developed countries today. It is rare everywhere in the third world.

'Hiatus hernia (an upward protrusion of the stomach through the diaphragm) has been shown by radiographic and endoscopic examination to be present in one in five adult Americans. I wrote a paper on hiatus hernia ten years ago. My co-editor was a man who had been the only thoracic surgeon in our teaching hospital in Africa for eight years. There he found not a single patient suffering from hiatus hernia. It is a disease of Western culture.

'Coronary heart disease kills one man in four in Britain. We did not see one case a year in our teaching hospital in Uganda, where the autopsy rate was over 50 per cent.

'Here is a quote from the standard medical textbook of 1920, the ninth edition of Ostler's *Principles and Practice of Medicine*: "Angina pectoris (angina for short) is a rare disease in hospitals. One case a year is about average, even in the large metropolitan hospitals in London."

'One patient a year! And yet today there are those who deal with this problem, so obviously due to modern Western culture, by giving people new hearts or plastic hearts. It is hard to think of anything more brilliantly irrelevant to the problem.

'Varicose veins is largely a disease of Western culture. In America a large survey showed that 50 per cent of all women over forty have them. A survey amongst 800 women in New Guinea found only one mild case. It is a Western disease. If you read textbooks you will find that varicose veins are caused by pregnancy, as if the human race had not yet adapted to getting pregnant.

'Five surveys in India, carried out by qualified surgeons, showed that varicose veins were more common in men than in women, and men don't get pregnant all that often!

'Diabetes (referring to the adult-onset type of diabetes mellitus) is common in Western communities but rare in rural communities in the third world. It is a recognized fact that certain individuals and ethnic groups are more likely to develop the disease than others.

'But irrespective of race the disease is rare in communities eating traditional foods. Conversely, it is one of the first of the Western diseases to emerge or increase in prevalence following changes of diet to a more Western pattern. It is significant that there is no diabetes in undomesticated animals. I am told no diabetes has yet been recorded in people who are hunter-gatherers, the most primitive people on earth.

'To give you an idea how life-style can alter diabetes, there is a little island in the Pacific called Nauru. It is only twelve miles around and probably not on your maps, but the Queen visited it last year, so it was on television. In 1952 its people had a very low level of diabetes just as most other Pacific islanders have. Then it was found that the island was covered with phosphates.

The islanders sold their phosphate and became the second richest people in the world, next to the oil-rich Arabs.

'They began looking at glossy magazines and saw what clever people the Americans and English were, with their hi-fi sets, radios and cars. They came to the erroneous conclusion that we knew what was best to eat. So they gave up their local food, changed to a more Western life-style and grossly over-ate. Now 40 per cent of the island's population over the age of twenty is diabetic and obesity is rampant.

'They have also learned how to get appendicitis; that starts early. They won't develop coronary heart disease or gall-stones for another twenty years, but they will come.

'Obesity is very much a disease of the Western culture. At the time of Cromwell England had an army of 40,000; English literature records that not one of them was fat. Obesity is today our major nutritional problem.

'Gall-stones is a disease of modern Western culture. It is estimated that a third of a million gall-bladders are removed annually in America. More is spent in the United States on taking out gall-stones than the total expenditure on preventive and curative health care in the whole continent of Africa. Yet it is largely a preventable disease.

'All of these diseases are as common now in black as in white Americans, and have similar prevalences in Americans of Japanese descent as in other ethnic groups, although they are relatively rare in Japan. The same applies to descendants of Pacific islanders now living in New Zealand. Moreover there is no evidence that any of these disorders was other than relatively rare, even in Western countries, before the present century.

'Epidemiological and other evidence thus indicates indisputably that these and other diseases are predominantly the result of Western life-styles. You cannot get away from that fact. Consequently they must be potentially preventable, if only the cause could be identified and reduced, or the factors which protect against them could be identified and enhanced.

'Here I want to make an important point about the danger of loose thinking. There is a world of difference between events being associated with one another and being causally related to one another. What you happen to be doing when you develop or recover from a disease is not necessarily the cause or the cure of the disease.

'Consider a rapidly growing town somewhere in Africa where the people have learned to develop obesity or appendicitis or diabetes. Somebody says: "We never saw appendicitis until we had plastic buckets. The more plastic buckets imported, the more appendicitis. Plastic buckets must be the cause of appendicitis." Or: "We never saw diabetes until we imported brief-cases. We think brief-cases are the cause of diabetes."

'We need more evidence than just relationships. Rather than considering plastic buckets or brief-cases we should consider changes in diet. All the diseases I have mentioned, without exception, are related directly or indirectly with the alimentary tract. And the environment of your gut and mine is determined by the food we eat.

'If we compare the third-world countries, where all these diseases are at a minimum, with Western countries where they are at a maximum, what do we find? As a percentage of energy, protein intake is fairly constant at around 11-14 per cent in most communities. In the third world it is largely derived from vegetables, whereas in the West it is mainly from animals.

'Protein intake in Britain and America has hardly altered in the past 100 years, the period over which these diseases have emerged. So I'll not spend time on proteins.

'As people get Westernized they always reduce their carbohydrate intake. Nearly half the carbohydrate intake in Britain now is sugar. There has been a catastrophic drop in starch. We get only about 30 per cent of our energy from starch, whereas the third world gets nearly 80 per cent of its energy this way. If you want to live a long and healthy life, get far more of your energy from starch: bread, flour products, cereals, beans and peas and root vegetables, particularly potatoes.

'Reduced starch intake is always accompanied by an increase in fat. We eat three times more fat than communities with a minimum prevalence of the diseases I have listed. We must reduce our fat. If I were a benevolent Czar and I could make a few edicts, one of them would be to abolish french fries. If you don't like your neighbour, then give him your frying-pan!

'The biggest nutritional catastrophe in this country in the past 100 years had been the deliberate removal of fibre. We did not understand its nature or properties and had no way of measuring them. We thought it was cellulose. We gave it to the cattle. Third-world countries eat 60-140 grams of fibre a day. We usually eat under 20 grams. As a result our stool output has dwindled. We have a laxative industry in this country only because we have taken the fibre out of our food. We have got to get it back.

'One way is the poor, humble, magnificent potato, said to be second only to the egg as the most complete food. It is a fallacy that potatoes are fattening. Potatoes have almost the same calorie value, weight-for-weight, as apples and are never fattening provided, and here comes the crunch, they are neither cooked in fat nor eaten with fat.

'I was lecturing to a group in Galway last September. Three doctors came up to me afterwards and reminded me that as students they had participated in a trial I had been involved in about ten years ago. They were among twenty-three students who undertook to eat two pounds of potatoes a day for three months.

'They were allowed to eat other things but after ten large potatoes you don't have much taste for the fattening foods. The aim of the trial was to see the effect of potatoes on bowel behaviour. I am told that the young men passed the best stools seen in Galway for a long time. The interesting thing was, most of them lost weight. So get back to potatoes!

'We have also drastically reduced our grain consumption. In England we are nearly at the bottom of the European bread-eating league, eating about a quarter of a pound of bread a day each. Our ancestors ate about a pound and a half. Until very recently only 10 per cent of our bread was brown or wholemeal. Things are getting better. In Holland it is now over 50 per cent. In Denmark it is over 70 per cent.

'So eat more bread. If I could advise one change in your diet to improve your health it would be to eat two to three times as much bread. Not white. But brown or wholemeal.

'What does fibre do to your gut and mine? I can only touch on it briefly tonight. If you put fibre into a glass of water, what happens? It absorbs water and swells. In the gut fibre will hold the water partly by mechanical attraction and partly by providing food for the bacteria which are 80 per cent water anyway. So fibre ensures the presence of a large soft, easy-moving mass. It is strongly protective against constipation, and by this and other means provides protection against many diseases of the gut.

'There have been several revolutions in the treatment of diseases since fibre became understood. The first after constipation was diverticular disease. It used to be treated with a low-fibre diet. Now it is being treated everywhere with a high-fibre diet. Until recently diabetes was treated with a diet low in carbohydrates and high in fats. Now it is being treated by a diet high in starch, very high in fibre and low in fat. With both diseases the results of the new treatment have been marvellous.

'The approach to obesity has also been revolutionized. No longer is there a blanket restriction on carbohydrate. Starch and fibre are recommended, fat and sugar reduction recommended. Dietary changes now also play a prominent role in the treatment of haemorrhoids, and surgical treatment has become much less radical.

'Large bowel cancer has been a particular interest of mine for about fifteen years. It is generally believed that excess fat in the diet plays a role in causing large bowel cancer. It is now even more firmly believed that fibre in the diet provides protection against this disease, one of the commonest of all cancers in the West. How does fibre provide protection?

'Fibre in the diet makes the stool more acid. As a result there is less bacterial degradation of the normal bowel constituents into potential carcinogens (cancer-producing substances), so fibre probably reduces the carcinogens in your gut and mine. Also fibre increases the mass of the stool, so any carcinogens contained in it are beneficially diluted. In addition, intestinal transit time is shortened, so contact between carcinogens and the bowel lining is also shortened.

'Bowel and breast cancer have very similar epidemiological features. Both diseases are always either common or rare together. You may wonder why breast cancer should be related to fibre and stools. Recent studies have shown that the amount of oestrogen you get rid of in your stool is directly related to the size of the stool. And this is inversely related to the oestrogen level in your plasma.

'So the bigger your stool the lower your plasma oestrogen level. I'm not going to argue now how this links with breast cancer but we know that oestrogen is cancer-linked and that vegetarians get less breast cancer than non-vegetarians. Nevertheless, excessive fat is probably a more important factor in causing this tumour.

'Your chances of a long and healthy life are much more related to the amount of stool you pass than to your blood pressure or serum cholesterol levels. So ideally you should weigh your stools occasionally to see how much you pass each week! Most people are not prepared to do that. But there is another test you can apply.

'Communities with high-fibre diets tend to have large, floating stools. Western communities normally have small, sinking stools. Large, floating stools throughout the world are associated with low rates of colo-rectal and breast cancer and other Western diseases. Small, sinking stools are associated with high rates. This is because fibre increases gas formation in the bowel. Some of this is passed as flatus, and some is trapped in the stools, making them float.

'In America people spend endless money annually checking for early signs of bowel cancer and other diseases. Far better to protect yourselves from getting these diseases than to detect them early. You can find out tomorrow whether you are a floater or a sinker. And you will do yourself much more good by becoming and remaining a floater than by having frequent clinical tests, despite their advantages.

'And if you are a member of the medical profession: by doubling the size of Doncaster stools in the next decade you will do much more for the health of your community than if you double the number of hospital beds. And at a much lower cost.

'If we are going to conquer Western diseases, if a reduction is to be achieved, it will not be by improving treatment but by eradicating causes. And one of the causes I am emphasizing is a faulty diet.

'Let me illustrate my message by using a couple of cartoons drawn by my daughter Judy. Imagine a shelf fixed crookedly to a wall. The earthenware pots are sliding off and smashing on the floor. There are two ways of dealing with the problem. One is to hire a world authority on mending pots. He has just developed a new wonder glue which is better for mending pots than anything ever used before. Everyone is happy because they can all gain financially, especially the owner of the glue-making factory.

'Then comes along another man who straightens up the shelf. No longer are the pots sliding off. The pot-mender, poor fellow, is out of work. There is a general air of despondency because, although it is best for the pots, no one is going to make much money out of straightened shelves — and remember that you and I are the pots!

'Let me put it another way. Here we have water running from a tap. The basin is full to overflowing and there is a flood on the floor. Two highly dedicated, well-trained gentlemen have a single motive in life — to try to keep the floor dry. They mop fourteen hours a day, no time for wives or families. It never occurs to them it might be better to turn off the tap.

'The water from the tap represents the cause of the diseases that are potentially preventable and are filling our hospital beds. Half a century ago I spent five years as a medical student learning how to mop floors. When I qualified as a doctor I studied for post-graduate diplomas on the use of electronic mops and improved brushes. I mopped furiously and happily for thirty years before I began to look at the taps.

'If you go into any doctor's office in North America, which I often do, all four walls are plastered with framed testimonials of all the mopping courses he has attended. He is very good at it. Let me say, you must mop well, I hope you will all mop well.

There will always be a flood on the floor. But it is not much good mopping, unless you also do something to turn off the tap.

'Only by straightening shelves or turning off taps will we conquer our current non-infective diseases. Never by merely improving the glue or the methods of mopping. Yet in England today something like 99 per cent of health expenditure goes on floor-mopping. One per cent on prevention, on turning off taps. In America it is a third of one per cent. I sometimes wonder whether we don't deserve the comment made by that Baltimore poet, Ogden Nash, when he said: "We are making great progress but we are heading in the wrong direction." Unfortunately that is all too possible.'

CHAPTER 20

Triumph and Tragedy

One day, in January 1978, the phone rang at the Burkitts' Oxfordshire home. It was Peter Ashmore, Master of the Queen's Household. He had been commanded to invite Denis Burkitt to a luncheon to be given by the Queen and the Duke of Edinburgh at Buckingham Palace in two weeks' time.

Denis immediately assumed there had been some mistake. Surely the Queen had never heard of him. On the contrary, Vice-Admiral Sir Peter Ashmore assured him, the Queen knew of him and his work. Was he free on 15 February? Denis checked his diary. What important entry could possibly have kept him away from such an invitation? Yes, he was free.

For the two weeks that followed, the invitation remained a secret within the Burkitt household. Judy, Cass and Rachel were even more excited about it than their father. They teased him with the old nursery rhyme 'Pussy cat, pussy cat, where have you been?', knowing that he would soon be able to answer, 'I've been to London to visit the Queen.'

In due course the official invitation arrived. Denis had to be at Buckingham Palace at 12.50. It was his second visit. On the previous occasion, in 1974, he had been made a Companion of the Order of St Michael and St George, in recognition of his work in Africa. That day Rachel, who was then working in London, had insisted on taking her father there in her elderly Mini, just for the fun of driving in through the palace gates.

This time he walked the mile from his office at St Thomas's Hospital, where he had been Honorary Senior Research Fellow in the Unit of Geographical Medicine since leaving the

Medical Research Council two years earlier. He crossed Westminster Bridge and went up Birdcage Walk.

'When I left my office I still kept my luncheon appointment a secret. Had anyone asked me where was I going and I'd replied, "to the palace for lunch with the Queen", no one at the hospital would have taken me seriously.'

He remembers getting to the palace much too early and walking up and down Constitution Hill until it was time to present himself at the gates.

'The policeman checked my name off his list and I enjoyed walking across the courtyard, conscious of being stared at by eyes peering through the railings. I was met inside the palace by Sir Peter Ashmore and was introduced to the other luncheon guests. They represented a diversity of callings: Margaret Drabble, the authoress; J. Vernon Addison, Editor of the *Cumberland Evening News and Star*; Sir Ian Bancroft, Head of the Civil Service; Peter Godfrey, Professor of Music at Auckland University; Jack Hedley, the actor; Sir John Methven, Director-General of the CBI; The Rev. Mark Santer, Principal of Westcote House, Cambridge.'

After drinks, as Denis and the other guests, together with two members of the household staff, were ushered into the dining-room, he tried to take in as much as he could of the details. He knew that back home he would be showered with questions from the women of his family about flowers and furniture and decor. He made a mental note of it all, from the paintings on the walls, to the royal coat-of-arms on the silver and glassware.

After lunch, he and the other guests each had an opportunity to speak with the Queen and the Duke of Edinburgh. Denis was surprised to hear from the Duke that he had read and absorbed much of Cleave's book, *The Saccharine Disease*.

At 2.45 the Queen and the Duke retired. Denis left the palace and walked back to his office to carry on with his work. To an onlooker it would have been as though nothing special had happened. But for Denis it had been a memorable occasion; a highlight in a year in which he was to be honoured in several ways for his work.

Already he had received news that at the January Council

meeting of the British Medical Association it had been decided to award him their Gold Medal, the Association's highest award, for 'making one of the most remarkable discoveries in the history of cancer research', namely Burkitt's lymphoma. The citation for the medal explained how this discovery had 'opened one of the most exciting stories in cancer research with the possibility that the disease might be the first example known to man of a neoplasm (cancerous growth) started up in some way by a micro-organism carried by an insect. That part of the story is unfinished. What did reach a gratifying conclusion was the clinical part. You found that this fast-growing and previously fatal neoplasm was so susceptible to chemotherapy that complete cure could be achieved.

'For your work on what became known as Burkitt's lymphoma you were elected a Fellow of the Royal Society in 1972. In now conferring on you the Gold Medal of the British Medical Association, the Council honours a medical man who has set a shining example in a tradition established by illustrious predecessors — that of medical naturalist. But you passed beyond mere thought-provoking observations and succeeded in curing your young patients of a terrible disease.'

This award was publicly announced just three days after Denis's lunch at the palace. The very same day he also got a letter from the University of Bristol offering him an honorary degree of Doctor of Medicine. His diary entry contains the comment: 'I would rather it went to Hugh.'

In the submission to the Vice-Chancellor of Bristol University, Denis Burkitt's sponsor, his friend Professor Tony Epstein, carefully summarized the distinctions of Denis's career and then listed the acknowledgements he had thus far received as a result of those distinctions.

'I have told you about Dr Burkitt's progress through his career. Now I must say a word about the reactions of the world of science to his contributions:

'In 1964 the Harrison Prize from the Royal Society of Medicine; in 1966 the Stuart Prize from the British Medical Association; in 1968 the Arnott Gold Medal of the Irish Hospitals and Medical Schools Association; in 1969 the

Katherine Berkan Judd Award of the Sloane-Kettering Institute, New York; in 1970 the Robert de Villiers Award of the American Lukemia Society; in 1971 the Walker Prize from the Royal College of Surgeons of England; in 1972 the Paul Erlich Ludwig-Darmsdaeter Prize and Gold Medal (Germany), the London Society of Apothecaries' Gold Medal, and the Albert Lasker Clinical Chemotherapy Award (USA); in 1973 the Gairdner Foundation Award (Canada); and in 1978 the British Medical Association Gold Medal — each of these a major scientific accolade.

'And to match this catalogue let me tell you of the honours he has received from academic bodies. An honorary DSc of the University of East Africa in 1970; Fellowship of the Royal Society in 1972; Honorary Fellowship of the Royal College of Surgeons of Ireland in 1973; and Honorary Fellowship of the Royal College of Physicians of Ireland in 1976. He has been made an Honorary Fellow of the East African Association of Surgeons; of the Brazilian Society of Surgery; of the Sudan Association of Surgeons; and of the International Medical Club of Washington.'

One award Denis received in 1978 which was unlikely to find its way into any list of medical acknowledgements was the Blocksma Award, created that year in honour of his friend the plastic surgeon, Ralph Blocksma. Denis was its first recipient.

This award was different from all the others he had been offered, in that its primary aim was to give recognition to the Christian motivation behind all that Denis had achieved in his medical work. It had been created by MAP International, the medical aid organization which had been so helpful to Denis with his world-wide questionnaires.

Denis and Olive had been friends of the Blocksmas ever since they had first met in Mulago in 1962, the year of Uganda's independence. Ralph and Ruth and Denis and Olive had visited each other's homes several times. The two men had even been on safari in Africa together.

Ralph trained as a plastic surgeon and served in the American Army Medical Corps during the Second World War. Between 1949 and 1953 he worked with his wife and family in northern

India (now west Pakistan), where he founded the United
Christian Hospital in Lahore. Back home in America he was in
practice as a plastic and reconstructive surgeon. From 1966–69
and from 1971–74 he had been chairman of the board of MAP
International.

The presentation to Denis of the Blocksma Award took place
early in June 1978, at the eighth International Convention of
Missionary Medicine at Wheaton College, on the outskirts of
Chicago. The award and plans for its presentation had been
kept a complete secret from Ralph, who afterwards described it
as a 'mountain-top experience'.

For Denis, who knew of it in advance, this award gave him
particular pleasure because of his close friendship with Ralph,
while causing him embarrassment. He had first heard about it
three months earlier, at the beginning of an eight-day lecture
tour in America. The first morning there, the phone in his hotel
room woke him early.

'It was Ray Knighton, telling me about the setting up of the
award and about how my name had been put forward as the
first recipient.'

The news worried Denis and through the day as he set out for
his first lecture venue it was uppermost in his mind. How could
he accept such an award with his 'minimal contribution'?

That night he slept badly and the following morning was up
early. He had decided he must decline the offer. By 5.30 a.m.
he had written to Ray telling him of his decision and suggesting
several other possible recipients.

But Denis had not reckoned with his old friend's ability to get
his own way. Back home in England the week after his tour,
Denis received Ray's reply.

'In the letter he told me there was no prospect of getting the
MAP board together again in time and if I refused the award
then it would not be given at all, which would be a huge
disservice to Ralph. Since there was hardly anyone I would
rather see honoured than Ralph, I had no choice but to submit
to his wishes.'

In the September of 1978, while still keeping his honorary
appointment at St Thomas's Hospital, Denis vacated his office.

It was wanted for other uses and he was finding less and less need for it. At the same time Denis and Olive moved from their home in Shiplake. All three girls were now married, with homes of their own. Six bedrooms were too many for their needs and Denis felt they should have a place that was less expensive to run.

For the past two years, almost since Denis had left the Medical Research Council, they had been looking for another house, but without any success. Then one day Judy rang to say that a friend was selling a house only three miles from where she and her husband Philip were living in Gloucestershire and it would be ideal for them.

So, before the end of the year, they had moved into their new Cotswold home, an eighteenth-century house built of mellow sandstone with two acres of garden, overlooking the wooded slopes of the Toadsmoor Valley.

Although the move to the Cotswolds greatly increased the travelling distance to Heathrow, it did nothing to curb Denis's international travel. Four trips a year to America to lecture, mostly on the perils of Western ways of life and diet, continued to be the norm. Nor was there any decline in the public recognition given to Denis's medical work and Christian service. In fact some of his most valuable acknowledgements, those from his medical and academic peers, were still to come.

In 1979 his work was recognized in two very different but equally pleasurable events. His own university, Trinity College, Dublin, conferred on him its highest honour, the Honorary Fellowship of Trinity College. Only two other living medical doctors hold this title.

In the same year the Christian Medical Society of the USA invited him to their annual conference of delegates in San Antonio, Texas. Here he was presented with their first 'Servant of the Year' award, a ceramic replica of a bowl, draped with a towel and standing on a wooden plinth. It symbolized Christ's washing of his disciples' feet, as one who came to serve.

The best year of all following his move was 1982. That year he received the two most prestigious international awards for cancer research — the Bristol-Myers Award and the Mott

General Motors Award — and was awarded an honorary Doctorate of Science by Leeds University.

The Bristol-Myers Award was made jointly to Denis Burkitt and to Professor Tony Epstein for the work they had done in discovering and establishing the importance of the virus that became known as the Epstein-Barr Virus. The two men were the first non-Americans to be given the award. Although Denis had gone on to other areas of research a decade before, Tony Epstein had continued with it.

To give publicity to the Bristol-Myers Award in both the country of the donors and the country of the recipients, its presentation was in two parts. First there was a press reception in London, at Chandos House.

'The beautiful surroundings,' recalls Denis, 'the flower arrangements and sumptuous reception were about as great a contrast as could be imagined to the circumstances in which most of my work had been done. What gave me most satisfaction was that Tony Epstein and I were able to emphasize to the assembled press the enormous importance of the complementary nature of the totally different and distinctive contributions we had been able to make to the same field of research. Our continuing friendship was also underlined, for harmonious relationships between people are the essence of all team endeavour.'

Within a week Denis and Olive were on their way, together with Tony, to New York. They flew first class, which worried Denis. Surely the £1,800 their two tickets cost could have been put to better use, if they had been allowed to travel economy? In fact he had written to Bristol-Myers suggesting just that, and asking that some of the money saved be sent to a missionary friend in Africa.

His suggestion was not taken up. So, for the first time in their lives, Denis and Olive were travelling together in first-class luxury. As he settled down for the flight Denis could not help pondering on the fact that their flight was costing someone £2 a minute.

'Long before the seat-belt signs had been turned off we had cost our sponsors many times the value of my total research grant for the first eighteen months of the project for which I was about to be honoured.'

At Kennedy Airport they were met by a chauffeur who drove them in an enormous Lincoln Continental to the Waldorf Astoria Hotel.

Next day Olive and Denis sat in their luxury hotel room overlooking the streets of Manhattan and reminisced about the third-rate hotel in which they had stayed during their first visit together to Dublin, and the back-street pension from which, many years earlier on their way back from Uganda, they had explored Florence.

For Denis the memory which provided the greatest contrast was a night in a rest-house on the shores of Lake Nyasa, spent with the Blocksmas on safari. In that place the stay had been enlivened by the bat-droppings falling on them from a tattered hessian ceiling.

'Now we laughed at our luxury, wondering at the way our paths had led to that day, humbly thanking God for all his goodness and mercy to us as a family.'

After a series of press and television interviews, the day of the presentation arrived. That morning Denis had been reading in his New Testament the story of Christ's transfiguration, of how the cloud enveloping the disciples had blotted out the world, as they heard God's voice. Denis wrote in his diary that day: 'The clamour, claims and consciousness of material pressures and pursuits stifle the voice of God.'

He took this as a warning of the dangers of the congratulations and adulation that of necessity are part of any award-giving ceremony.

There were 400 people at the presentation. Amongst the old friends Denis and Olive were able to meet once again were some who had been at the Burkitt Lymphoma Conference, which Denis had organized just before he and his family had left Uganda in 1966.

In his acceptance speech, Denis referred to his continuing amazement that his first steps in cancer research, searching for the cause of a child's lymphoma, had blossomed into such an important enterprise as the discovery of the EB virus. It seemed to him, as he recalled the summer holidays at Laragh with his brother Robin, that it was like a small boy gathering sticks for a fire to boil a kettle.

'Should another boy come along and pour on paraffin to fan the flames and cause a forest fire, the blame for the destruction would be on the one who fanned the flames, not on the boy who lit the fire. My little fire had been blown up into a spreading blaze by Tony Epstein and others. Just as the flame fanner deserves the blame, so the fanners of the flames which resulted in the discovery of the EB virus deserve the credit.'

The day after the presentation Denis and Olive flew back to Heathrow, again first class. Here they were met by a chauffeur with a British limousine just as big as the American one. They were driven back to their home in the Cotswolds, arriving there at 1.30 a.m., tired but grateful and happy.

Six weeks after returning from America Denis went with Olive, Judy and Judy's husband Philip to Leeds University for the conferment of his honorary Doctorate of Science. The ceremony was in marked contrast to the Bristol-Myers presentation.

With the former the emphasis was on a monetary prize donated by an international commercial organization. Consequently it was conducted in an atmosphere of massive publicity and flashing cameras. Pre-briefed members of the press were an integral part of the entire event, which afterwards had coverage in more than sixty American and twenty British newspapers.

By contrast, the honorary degree ceremony was totally devoid of any hint of publicity. Not a single camera flash was to be seen and the question of money never raised its head.

Six honorary degrees were conferred that day. The other five were to: Professor Le Roy-Lalurde of the University of Paris; Miss Jacqueline Du-Pré, the cellist; Sir Henry Chilvers, Vice-Chancellor of Cranfield Institute of Technology; Sir Derek Ezra, then Chairman of the National Coal Board; Lord Hailsham; and Sir Rudolf Lyons, QC.

What made the occasion particularly exciting for Denis and Olive was the fact that the University Chancellor conferring the degrees was the Duchess of Kent. Twenty-two years previously, Her Royal Highness with her husband had represented the Queen at Uganda's independence ceremonies and Denis Burkitt had been their official medical advisor.

Three weeks after the conferment at Leeds, Denis and Olive were off again to New York, this time for Denis to receive the General Motors Mott Award for his work on Burkitt's lymphoma. Again they were met by limousine at Kennedy Airport and driven to their Manhattan hotel.

It was some relief to Denis that press coverage was less ostentatious than on the previous visit. There were limited press interviews and just one television interview. Then it was off to Washington for the main events, the presentation of the awards to Denis and to two American doctors.

It was the first time Denis had ever worn a black tie and dinner jacket in America. The Union Jack had been placed between two American flags. The presentation of the gold medals was made: the two American doctors had standing by their sides the congressmen representing the states in which they worked; Denis Burkitt had a senior official of the British Embassy.

Denis was most impressed with the way the event was organized:

'The whole occasion was conducted throughout with dignity, thoughtfulness and generosity. When I consider the awards I have received this year alone I am ashamed to think that I ever imagined that I was making a sacrifice when I left home to go to Uganda.'

In the midst of all the awards and honours of 1982 an event took place in the Burkitt family that put them all into perspective. It is a story best told in Denis's own words.

'Our youngest daughter Rachel, and her doctor husband David, had been looking forward with joyful anticipation to the birth of their first child after five years of marriage. The little one arrived a month prematurely on Saturday night, to flood us with heart-felt thankfulness.

'Judy and Philip invited us to share lunch with their family the following day, so we could rejoice and be together. Halfway through the meal the phone rang. It was Rachel calling Judy. Only a few words were said. No more was needed to pierce our hearts and stun us all.

'Edward, the new baby, was a mongol, a Down's syndrome baby. Too shocked to speak, we sat silently gazing at our half-empty plates. Silent tears began to flow. Judy was the first to break the stillness. I can't remember exactly what she said. But the gist was that everything was in the hands of our loving God and that apparent tragedies can be turned into triumphs.

'As the news spread we were overwhelmed with messages of sympathy, love and understanding. Letters and long-distance calls came from many people. Some broke down as they tried to speak. Edward's arrival brought out the best in people.

'We began to feel part of an event that could be used by God as a channel of blessing to countless people. It had happened before. The shameful and agonizing death of Jesus, the Son of God, on a criminal's cross brought untold blessings to multitudes. "God had chosen the weak things of the world to confound the mighty." So it would be with Edward.

'Edward's second name was to have been Burkitt but, when it was realized that he was unlikely to have a family, Rachel and David decided to call him Samuel, "Gift of God".

'The story of little Edward has the beneficial effect of putting other happenings in life into perspective.

'Ultimately that which is unseen takes priority over the seen, the eternal over the temporal. Intangible qualities of love, peace, sympathy and acceptance of sacrifice take precedence over intelligence, competence and apparent achievement.

'One month after the birth of Edward, I read in Matthew's Gospel: "You will be arrested and tried and whipped . . . This will give the opportunity to tell them about me." Jesus was telling his disciples that suffering provides the opportunity to tell of God's love.

'The next day in the same chapter I read: "Don't be afraid of those who can kill only your bodies." Deficiencies in the body and mind are much less of an evil than a spirit in rebellion against God in a healthy body.

'When Edward was two months old Rachel put into words what we had all been feeling as a family. "When Jesus chose a vehicle to carry him into Jerusalem for the most important event in his life he deliberately picked a docile and stupid donkey. In the world's eyes Edward may be stupid but he can carry Jesus into the lives of others."

'I take every opportunity I get to express the conviction that prevention saves people from far more suffering than treatment, even though both must be pursued with honesty, and dedication. My interest in diet well illustrates another conviction. The removal of the outer coat of a wheat grain in order to extract the prized starch has been one of the major errors made in nutritional science. The carton has been rejected and attention focused on the content. But often science and medicine make the opposite mistake, investigating the biological framework (the carton) and overlooking the inner man (the content).

'A paralyzed man was carried to Jesus by a group of caring friends who sympathized with him because of his disability. They laid him at Jesus' feet. To their dismay, Jesus seemed to look through the diseased carton and concentrate on the needs of the person within.

'"Your sins are forgiven."

'At this stage the "contents" were healed but within a still-defective carton. His friends could see no improvement. To them his inner healing was irrelevant. To convince them that the cure was real, Jesus went on to heal the carton, the man's physical body.

'Olive and I thank God for the windows of hope opened by the birth of our grandchild who arrived in a defective carton. As a family we would not think of exchanging him for a "normal" child. We realize his potential as an instrument for God.'

Denis has always been convinced that the many pivotal occasions in his life, in particular his meetings with other people like Oéttle, Cleave, Walker and Trowell, have been providential rather than mere chance. This conviction he finds best expressed in a text from Paul's letter to the Corinthians, which hangs amongst the many honours and awards in his Cotswold study.

'What do you possess which you have not received and, if you receive it all as a gift, why take the credit to yourself?'

Author's acknowledgements

For their help to me in gathering material for Denis's fascinating story I am indebted to a number of people who know him well. Two in particular are his brother Robin and his very good friend Hugh Trowell. I am also grateful for the insight into the medical aspects of his work which I gained from the eminently readable work of two American medical writers: Bernard Glemser in *The Long Safari* and Lawrence Galton in *The truth about fibre in your diet*.

Thanks must also be expressed to *Today* magazine for permission to include an extract from Roger Day's interview, first published in what was then *Crusade*. And where would I have been without Denis's own gift for communicating so powerfully and yet humbly? If he has a fault it is his eagerness to talk about other people's work rather than his own. Thank you also, Olive, for your hospitality and home cooking.

Personally, the most important acknowledgement must go to my wife Val, without whose encouragement and loyalty this book would not have been finished. She has taught me that love can overcome all things.

Brian Kellock

Index